TEACHING & ASSESSING 21ST CENTURY COMPETENCIES

A PLANNING, RESOURCE AND REFERENCE WORKBOOK IN THE DEEPER LEARNING WORKSHOP SERIES

ENGAGEMENT, INNOVATION AND IMPACT BY DESIGN

PRINCIPAL AUTHOR:
Charity Allen

Produced by
PBL Consulting
936 NW 57th St
Seattle, WA 98107

Please contact
PBL Consulting at
www.pblconsulting.org,
360-440-3968 or
charity@pblconsulting.org
for more information.

GRAPHIC DESIGN BY:
Charity Allen

www.pblconsulting.org

21ST CENTURY COMPETENCIES
TABLE OF CONTENTS

CRITICAL THINKING

PRESENTATIONAL COMMUNICATION

INQUIRY

CREATIVE AGILITY ICEBREAKER

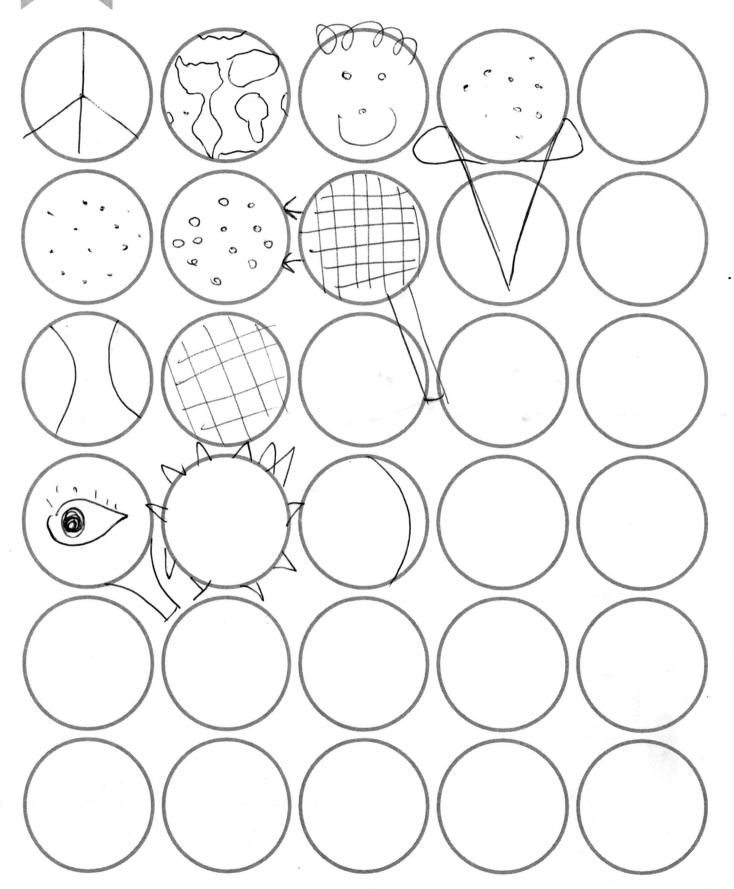

WHY, WHAT & HOW?

21st Century Competencies are viewed increasingly by employers, educators, families and by children themselves as being vital to flourishing in our lives both today, and beyond.

COLLABORATION

CREATIVITY & INNOVATION

4 Cs

CRITICAL THINKING

PRESENTATIONAL COMMUNICATION

Though not an exhaustive list of skills, this book will focus on the following four key competencies - the 4 Cs:
1. Collaboration
2. Creativity and Innovation
3. Critical Thinking
4. Presentational Communication.

You will find sections for each of these four competencies that begin with an "At-A-Glance" overview to provide foundational understanding and context. Then, in each section, you will find sets of resources for each of the four Cs intended to help you with "the how" behind scaffolding and explicitly developing these competencies. In addition to the resources found in the book, many are also freely available online at - www.pblconsulting.org - in the Free Resources section.

What Does It Mean to Teach & Assess the 4 Cs?

In a school setting, when working with youngsters, we can approach these competencies at various levels - ignore, encourage or actually teach and assess them.

IGNORE

ENCOURAGE

TEACH & ASSESS

On the minimalist end, we can completely ignore these competencies and choose not to actively develop them at all. Some teachers may default to this side of the spectrum out of a lack of awareness of the importance of developing these skills or perhaps because they feel there is insufficient time during the busy school day to both "cover the content" and to develop 21st Century Competencies.

In the middle, we can encourage competencies implicitly. I think encouraging is great, and well crafted learning experiences will absolutely encourage the development of the 4 Cs. That said, I would challenge you to tackle one of the 4 Cs per unit or per project, explicitly, at the teach and assess level.

On the far end, we can target, teach and assess one or more of the 4 Cs, explicitly. Teachers can design and facilitate high quality instruction and carefully crafted experiences to build capacity. This could include: scaffolding, structuring, teaching, modeling, prompting, framing, practicing, critiquing, reflecting and more. This book will help you reach the teach and assess level by building understanding around the why, the what and the how of each of the 4 Cs. It will also provide guidance and resources to support you in teaching and assessing as well as framing tasks that will encourage the development of the four Cs.

Think about all the projects and units you'll do throughout the year and try to tackle each of the 4 Cs at least once, with quality and depth. Great PBL experiences will to some degree encourage the four Cs, but could you go deeper with one?

WHY, WHAT & HOW?

 A Word of Caution: I have heard teachers who are new to Project Based Learning (PBL) say:

"Students are working in teams during this project, so that's collaboration."
"This project is really complex and so that's critical thinking.."
"Students are making something in this project, so that's creativity."
"At the end of the project, students are giving a presentation, so we are doing communication."

In each of those statements, the operating assumption is that expecting and/or assigning work that demands the 21st Century Competency is sufficient to teach it. Though I would ask, would we, as teachers, be so cavalier in the face of developing reading or writing skills? Or any of the other academic learning outcomes we target? Imagine for a second that I assigned students a narrative writing assignment and then explained that, "their narrative writing assignments are due at the end of the month, so we are 'doing narrative writing...'" Not so fast, right? Expecting is different than teaching. Though I believe high expectations are wildly important, those high expectations must be accompanied by great teaching and learning activities in addition to experiences that enable students to develop, practice and reflect upon their understandings, abilities and applications of each of the 4 Cs.

Teach One at a Time. A quick note on scope. You don't have to teach all 4 Cs in every single project or unit. In fact, it would be better to select one or two that can be targeted per unit or project. Imagine trying to teach three different types of writing - narrative, persuasive and informational - in the same unit. Could you do all three justice? It would definitely be a challenge. It would certainly spread a teacher thin without the right system in place. It could also turn into a logistical nightmare and then be cast to the side altogether. This is why the common practice is to tackle one strand of writing at a time. Perhaps we might do a flexible, self-directed project or unit toward the end of the year after students have had exposure to and support with multiple types of writing, wherein they could select their favorite type of writing. Though, this would be more common and more feasible after we'd built foundational capacity with students. The same could be said about the 4 Cs - tackle them one by one with a focus on quality over quantity.

Which of the 4 Cs Should I Pick?

Here are some rules of thumb:

 1. When in doubt, pick collaboration. Much of the work we do in great units and projects is hinged on successful collaboration. Thus, collaboration is my default.

2. Pick creativity and innovation if during the unit or project students will be producing original and novel products or services.

 3. Consider selecting presentational communication if your unit or project leads to students providing presentations to an authentic, public audience. This higher stakes forum for a presentation increases student motivation to *present well*. Students are less likely to value the quality of a presentation if it is only destined for a teacher's inbox or is only delivered to fellow students in class or in the school community.

 4. I believe critical thinking is the most challenging to teach and assess and I would recommend tackling it once you have begun to explicitly teach inquiry and feel like you could go deeper with the process of inquiry.

Why Collaborate? The fundamental rationale - the why - behind collaboration is the belief that we can build better ideas with the help of others than we could on our own. In a classroom, harnessing the collaborative capacity of individuals and teams can feel challenging at times. But it can be done.

Collaboration from the Ground Up

Fostering great collaboration is build on a foundation of two key components: knowledge of self and care for others. While that is an achievement in itself a team must also have collaboration-worthy work in order to have tasks to actually work on together. These first two tiers in the pyramid create the conditions for successful collaboration. At the top tier, efficient, productive and harmonious team interactions are typically governed with guidelines - every organization, and classroom has their own. Guidelines for team interactions can include: the use of roles, structures, norms protocols, processes, routines, tools, and more.

GUIDELINES FOR TEAM INTERACTIONS

COLLABORATION WORTHY WORK

KNOWLEDGE OF SELF   CARE FOR OTHERS

Build Foundations - Knowledge of Self

The ancient Greek aphorism: "know thyself" sums up this component of the bottom tier. To collaborate well with others, I must first understand myself - my personality, my tendencies with work and working with others, my strengths, my challenges, my preferences around learning and completing tasks and more. There are numerous tools that give individuals insights on themselves. They are powerful and fun to facilitate - after all, we tend to love learning and talking about ourselves. Popular tools include: StrengthsFinder, StengthsExplorer, Myers Briggs Personality Test, True Colors, the Personality Compass, Multiple Intelligences, Internal versus External Thinking and even the 5 Love Languages - yes folks, the 5 Love Languages. If it can save marriages, then it can build better teams in the classroom. While there is indeed power in continuity, it can be enlightening for students to use multiple tools over time to add new dimensions of understanding and insights into themselves. At the start of each new unit or project, we'd tackle a new tool and then represent our new data points on a new name tag, teacher included.

Build Foundations - Care for Others

The goal is to get students to the point that they would say the following about their team mates: "I know who they are as a person, I like them, I trust them and ultimately I care about their well being." To get there, it's necessary to engage individuals and teams in activities that build care for others. No, not trust falls and the like. In the face of inevitable team conflict, protocols are amazing tools. However, it's hard to imagine that a given problem solving approach or a conflict resolution protocol would achieve much more than shallow, superficial solutions without clear personal investment in the individuals with whom we work. Hence the importance of building genuine understanding of and care for others.

Well executed advisory programs can include effective activities and processes to build understanding and care for others. In the absence of an advisory program, or something comparable, teachers often harness the benefits of activities intended to learn more about self to build understanding of others.

I also love the use of lanyards and name tags that were created by kids and worn daily in class to visually project whichever inventories, aspects of learning profiles and personal interest surveys we were using. For example, a student's love language, an area of interest, an element of their learning style and a wild card of something personal they'd like to share. Each time we started a new project, we would use new inventories or reuse old data points and they would create a new name tag for themselves or we would have a rapid design challenge to create a name tag for their peers as a mechanism to help them get to know one another. In this way, whenever students interact with one another they have immediate insights into each other. Very quickly, they learn to flex and adapt in the face of the needs of others. I believe that's where collaboration starts to get more sophisticated, when an individual intentionally adapts to meet the needs of others in order to collaborate better.

Create Conditions - Collaboration-Worthy Work

Imagine a team of individuals who have strong knowledge of themselves and legitimate care for one another. We might feel a sense of assurance that great collaboration is inevitable. However, the team will still fail to reach deep levels of collaboration if we fail to frame challenges, projects and tasks that are "Collaboration-Worthy" - meaning difficult enough to require collaboration, open-ended and perceived as relevant to the team. Pedagogies for Deeper Learning - like Project/Challenge/Problem Based Learning can become a framework in which to design and facilitate rich, meaningful and empowering learning experiences for students, and for teachers, in which collaboration is necessary. This creates a platform to allow students to practice, reflect and improve in addition to their collaborative efforts being fruitful.

Establish Guidelines for Team Interactions - Norms, Structures & Processes

Highly collaborative environments often use roles, areas of focus, job descriptions, teams, groups and even teams within teams and more. (*See page 11 for common roles*). This can allow for distributed leadership and distributed expertise that can create a more collaborative environment. Roles are recommended at the secondary level and sometimes used at the primary level. Teams can last the duration of a project or be short-term, based on a task. Teams can be taught and given opportunities to set norms and practice protocols for more harmonious and productive interactions. Common team interactions include: discussion, ideation, reflection, communication, task delegation, task completion, decision making, conflict resolution, giving and receiving feedback, tuning work and more. This book contains pages of protocols to guide these interactions. These protocols can be taught, modelled and practiced to build collaborative capacity. Successful team interactions are indicators of collaboration-in-action.

> PROTOCOL: A set of rules governing how to conduct a task, e.g. decision making, discussion, reflection, etc. This usually includes a combination of several of the following: procedures, steps, time limits, guidance, norms, frames, dos and don'ts, facilitation guidelines, tips and more. With the use of protocols, we can achieve tasks in a more effective, efficient and harmonious manner.

Empower Harmonious and Productive Collaboration by developing capacity at each level of the triangle - building foundational understandings, creating working conditions and establishing guidelines for norms, structures and process.

PROTOCOLS FOR TEAM MEETINGS

PROTOCOLS FOR Team Meetings

Meetings can use useful tools during projects to harness collaboration and insight on a project-in-development. However, not all meetings are created equal. Meetings can also be overused, under productive and a waste of time. Use the following steps to plan for effective, productive and efficient meetings.

Select Meeting Leader(s)

Who will lead and guide the meeting? Will different leaders guide different parts of the same meeting? Do you rotate leaders for different meetings?

Determine Objectives

What do you hope to accomplish by the end of the meeting? Is a meeting really necessary to achieve these goals?

Set Reasonable Time Frames

Rarely should an official meeting last longer than 60 minutes. Can your objectives be completed in that period of time? Are you prepared to task delegate and re-meet? Once you have a reasonable time, create a schedule, share your schedule and stick to your schedule.

Invite Relevant Attendees

Think carefully about who needs to attend a meeting both to (1) actively participate and also possibly for (2) transparency and input. No one wants to feel excluded from important work, and conversely no one wants to feel compelled to attend a meeting at which their presence is unnecessary.

Create Meeting Norms or Use Protocols

To get as much done as possible, meeting leaders should be prepared to use norms or protocols to ensure active, even and fair participation from attendees. Norms can also include agreements made around technology usage during a meeting. E.g. Cell phones, laptops, etc.

End Meetings with Appreciation & Next Steps

Meetings can be intensely productive and highly collaborative. Ensure people feel their contributions were valued and appreciated. Meetings often end with additional tasks to be completed beyond the meeting. Make sure everyone can articulate their next steps and any deadlines.

COMMON TEAM ROLES

Below are some common team roles used in projects from grades 4-12. They can be written and treated like job descriptions.

Team Leader

- Establishes and runs team meetings
- Sets and monitors goals & agreements and redirects team, as needed
- Delegates tasks and divides work, as needed
- Mediates conflict between team members
- Encourager

Key Trait:
Relationship-oriented

Research Lead

- Goes outside of provided materials to gather and share useful information.
- Focuses on "supporting on the sidelines"
- Helps team overcome obstacles and roadblocks.
- Collects, maintains and uses the Team Need to Know List to drive work

Key Trait:
Resourceful

Organizational Lead

- Keeps time during activities and phases of design
- Maintains a schedules and tracks progress toward goals and milestones
- Keeps track of materials
- Organizes and maintains team documents

Key Trait:
Detail-oriented

Design Lead

- Directs team to use the design process.
- Tracks team's use of each phase of design
- Gathers team perspectives, makes key design decisions

Key Trait:
Process-oriented

Archivist

- Archives team's work in progress, drafts and prototypes
- Takes photos and videos of work in progress
- Captures quotes, moments & process

Key Trait:
Reflective

Curator

- Focuses on how work will be displayed at the end
- Pays attention to detail without losing sight of the big picture
- Collaborates with other curators to ensure continuity of work curating at the end
- Consults with team on during project

Key Trait:
Visionary

In addition to these "generic" roles, ask yourself: "If I was a professional in industry creating a comparable tangible outcome to the students in this project, what would my job be? What would my title be? What would some of the key elements of my job description be?" Could the answers to those questions help you frame a role for your specific project?

Professional Title:

Job Description: **Key Duties:**

PROTOCOLS FOR DECISION MAKING

PROTOCOLS FOR
Decision Making

Reaching agreement doesn't always happen organically, on it's own. Sometimes reaching agreement in a team on a method, process or protocol for making decisions can increase productivity, speed of work and prevent conflict.

DEMOCRATIC VOTING

Multiple (more than 2) options to be voted on. More than 4 people voting. One vote per person. May the best option win.

POLLS & SURVEYS

Polls and surveys can be useful when outside input is desired for decision making. If needed, polls and surveys can solicit the input of a focus group or representative sample. A poll may lead to the best decision, despite the fact that  the outcome of the polled audience may differ from the preferences of the team.

This can be useful in engineering and design of consumer goods wherein the inherent preferences of the engineers or designers are less relevant to the decisions to be made about the project.

CONSENSUS

Consensus is general or universal agreement. This means everyone participating in the decision making process has agreed on the same decision to be made. While consensus is often desired, it can be difficult to achieve. Consensus can be important when large decisions are being made in small groups. It can be very difficult, though not impossible, to reach in medium groups. Without time and extensive use of protocols, consensus may be unrealistic to use in large-group decision making.

BORDA METHOD OF VOTING

The Borda method is useful when voting is desired, but the group is too small for a clear "winner" to emerge. Many use Borda when there are fewer than five options on which to be voted and there are less than 8 people voting. Borda uses a ranking system, examples shown below.

Rank your choices in order, the highest indicating your top choice. Each voting member casts their "ranked votes." The option with the highest total tally becomes the "winning choice."

				Total Votes
Penguin	4	2	3	9
Lion	3	4	1	8
Cat	1	1	4	6
Dolphin	2	3	2	7

PERSON 1
Penguin	4
Lion	3
Cat	1
Dolphin	2

PERSON 2
Penguin	2
Lion	4
Cat	1
Dolphin	3

PERSON 3
Penguin	3
Lion	1
Cat	4
Dolphin	2

PROTOCOLS FOR CONFLICT RESOLUTION

MEDIATION

A variety of processes for mediation, including peer mediation, exist. Procedures and protocols for mediation can be useful when implemented consistently within a system.

PROTOCOLS FOR
Conflict Resolution

We can achieve more in teams than we can on our own. However, with collaboration sometimes comes conflict. Resolving conflict quickly and constructively can help prevent disharmony, dysfunction, rifts and grudges.

CONFLICT RESOLUTION SPEAK

This can be taught and used organically on an ongoing basis. It can also be a part of a larger protocol for conflict resolution. This is used in responsive classrooms. Find out where you can learn more about this process in the recommended content section.

When you....
I feel....
because....

GIRAFFE LANGUAGE

This protocol for sharing constructive feedback and solving conflict guides conversations through multiple stages: Invitation, observation, apology, appreciation, consequences, objectives and requests.

prompt

CHALK TALK

In this protocol, a word, phrase, question or prompt is written on a chalk board (or white board or butcher paper, etc.) and in silence students approach the chalk board and respond in writing. Their responses can connect to the initial prompt or they can connect directly to other responses. Multiple students can respond simultaneously. Students can respond multiple times. It ends when it ends. The entire protocol is silent.

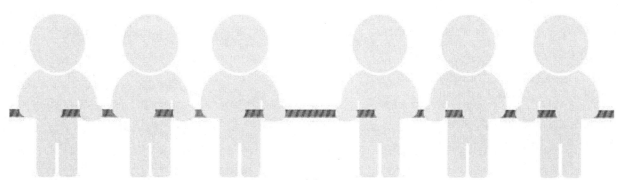

FISHBOWL

The protocol uses two concentric circles to create an inner circle and an outer circle. The protocol can be used for discussion or reflection. Those seated in the inner circle discuss a topic or prompt and those seated in the outer circle listen, observe, take notes or complete other designated tasks. Often an empty seat is placed in the inner circle. This "hot seat" modification can allow multiple outer circle participants to join the inner circle discussion temporarily.

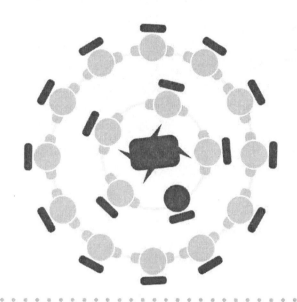

3, 2, 1 REFLECTION PROMPT

You can write any 3 questions or prompts. Students provide 3 responses to the first, 2 to the second and one to the final. Usually the first question or prompt is easier and lends itself to multiple responses and the final question or prompt is more complex.

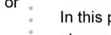

CHALK TALK

In this protocol, a word, phrase, question or prompt is written on a chalk board (or white board or butcher paper, etc) and in silence students approach the chalk board and respond in writing. Their responses can connect to the initial prompt or they can connect directly to other responses. Multiple students can respond simultaneously. Students can respond multiple times. It ends when it ends. The entire protocol is silent.

SUCCESS ANALYSIS PROTOCOL

This protocol is all about determining cause and effect. When someone experiences a profound success, this protocol can help uncover that which led to the success. i.e. cause and effect. The idea is that through the identification and analysis of causal factors, promoting subsequent "successes" will be more likely. Learn more about how to conduct this protocol at www.nrsfharmony.org

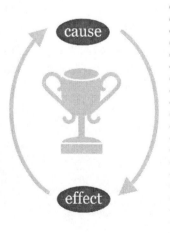

DISCUSSION & REFLECTION PROTOCOLS

WORLD CAFE

In this protocol for discussion, each table is assigned a topic, with a discussion prompt. Participants select the table and topic of their choice and discuss the topic and prompt for 5-10 minutes. Participants switch tables 3-4 times, selecting their top topics. It can feel a bit like "musical chairs," but with enough rotations, one usually gets their top choices of topics by the end. At each table, using chart or butcher paper, groups attempt to create a visual representation of their discussion, with minimal usage of words. Groups review and build on previous discussion visuals and share their final one.

CONTINUUM DIALOG

This protocol could be adapted to be used with students for discussion or reflection. In this protocol, an affirmative and negative statement are posed. Participants physically stand on a continuum. The continuum is indicated physically in the room as an arc in order for all participants to see where others place themselves. Placement on the continuum reveals participants' positions in regards to the posed statements. Once participants have placed themselves on the continuum the facilitator can ask them to explain (2 mins or less) why they placed themselves where they did. No rebuttals, no arguments, no judgment.

As participants listen and hear different perspectives, they can physically move themselves in the event that their perspective shifts.

Learn more about how to facilitate this protocol at www.nrsfharmony.org

QUESTIONS FOR REFLECTION

Common questions could include:

1. What have you learned from doing this project?

Content	Process

2. On a scale of 1-4, how difficult was this project? Explain...
3. What have you learned about yourself?

As A Learner	As A Team Member

4. What would you do differently in future projects and why?

Formative Critique, Tuning & Assessment

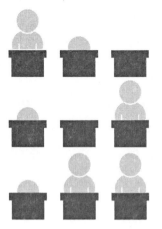

WHACK-A-MOLE PROTOCOL

Place student work, along with criteria, critique instructions and/or questions for reflection, at student desks and/or stations. Students move around, as space is available, to provide critique for multiple pieces of work.

The idea is that they pop up when they finish each critique, like a mole in the "Whack-A-Mole" game. Then, they pop back down in a new spot to conduct another critique, wherever one is available. This works well when the amount of time it will take to conduct critique will predictably vary.

CHARETTE PROTOCOL

This protocol was typically used in engineering. It is best used early on to feed-forward, rather than back. As soon as a process stalls, students can call a "charette" to get fresh perspectives and ideas on how to move their project forward.

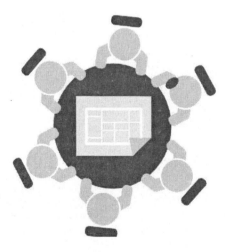

EXIT SLIPS

Prepared in advance by the teacher or done on-the-fly, exit slips can act as a check for understanding and/or collect information on work completion, effectiveness of instruction, process, materials, and more.

2 STARS & A WISH

Students can acknowledge and share 2 things that were done well. Then they share a wish they have that would enhance the work being examined.

PAIR CRITIQUE

Students are paired with a critique partner. Pairs respond directly to critique and feedback questions generated by the teachers, the class and/or by the work author or designer.

Formative Critique, Tuning & Assessment

GALLERY WALK

Text-lite work is hung in a space to mimic a "gallery." Participants walk the gallery and offer written feedback (often on Post-It Notes) in response to a prompt and/or using generic critique language.

INSTRUCTIONAL CRITIQUE

The teacher (or students) lead a small group or the whole class in the critique of one or more work samples to distil the quality indicators of said work. E.g. Thesis statements. The indicators can then be used to assess the students' work in progress. E.g. Students' draft thesis statements.

DILEMMA PROTOCOL

Student(s) present a dilemma, e.g. getting stuck, encountering a tricky problem, writer's block, etc. and protocol participants offer constructive feedback about how to respond to the dilemma.

ABC OF A TEXT

Create a acronym, each letter asks students to look for something specific in the work being examined.
e.g. SLUG

    S - Spelling

    L - Letter Formation

    U - Uppercase (first letter of first word in sentence)

    G - Greatness (what's great about the work)

COLLABORATION RESOURCES
STRATEGIES TO FORM TEAMS

Whether it's your 1st PBL project or your 50th - there are always surprises. The role of a constructivist PBL teacher is to curate a space in which that variation can flourish while still providing and facilitating an effective learning environment for a diverse group of students.

It's the first week of school and you're thrilled to introduce a new project to students. You've identified learning targets, planned out lessons and activities, and have a stack of handouts ready to go. Before you can finish your first sentence a hand shoots up.

"Mr. Swaaley - is this a group project?"

You proudly explain that yes, this is a group project in which we will model real world experiences through peer collaboration and the meaningful development of peer relationships. The student nods and you continue to explain the project. Seconds later another hand shoots up.

"Mr. Swaaley - how are we choosing groups?"

You then explain that either groups will be assigned or that they will be self-selected through wise partner choices. Instantly, even silently, students start the partner courting process and the rest is history.

We've all been in a situation like this as both a learner and an educator. It never feels good. We teachers lose the focus of the class, feel like whatever we say will elicit backlash, know that parent emails are imminent, and worry about that one kid in every group that gets screwed. Students get caught in strange social obligations, feel like the last kid to be picked to play dodgeball, and are often forced to make awkward and immediate public choices. Is there a better way?

Grouping is often the first thing students ask about. This shows how relevant it is to the student experience and I would argue that it's the most immediate and clearly defining characteristic of the project experience. Every student deserves to be challenged by work within their Zone of Proximal Development in a safe and supportive environment. The formation of groups is a contentious process for both students and parents. Everyone is bringing in baggage. Now let's apply those understandings to a few grouping methods and see what we come up with.

Method 1 - Hot Potato

This method works well if you have some familiarity with the students at the start of a project. If you don't know them well enough yet, you can enlist another teacher to help evaluate or give them a randomly grouped mini-project (a few days) to let you assess how they work with others and their competency in the subject. Even if you don't know the students, this method can still be helpful.

Have a conversation with the class about things to consider when deciding who to work with (see ideas below).

18

STRATEGIES TO FORM TEAMS

Hand out index cards and have students document the following on the lined side of the index card:

(1) Their name in large letters on the top,
(2) a list of three people they would like to work with, each identified with a '+' sign, on the right,
(3) a list of two people they do not want to work with, each identified with a '-' sign, on the left, and
(4) a brief note if there's anything they want to let you know.

They turn these into you privately and confidentially.

Outside of class, you lay all of the cards out on a table and shuffle them around to find copacetic groupings that accommodate as much student preference as possible, keeping an eye out for known distractors, gender balance, and skill balanced groups.

Before you give out groupings, chat about the importance of first impressions (i.e. no "groans", "yehaws", or whispers as group mates are announced.) You present the groupings to the class at the next meeting.

This method works well for a number of reasons:

(1) Students are pretty good at making wise choices for themselves if the decision process is private. You'll be surprised how many students put their best friend as someone that they DO NOT want to work with.

(2) Giving students a real choice, or at least a preference, empowers them to make better decisions and feel more personally accountable and willing to fix anything that goes awry.

(3) This gives students a back-door to remove themselves from unproductive groups when a more public selection process may have made it more socially awkward. As far as they know - the groups are entirely self-selected (wink.)

Variations to the Hot Potato Method:

If the cards don't align into tidy groups (which can and will happen), engage students in the process. Pull a student aside or email them a quick note to the effect of "Hey, Billy, I know you really wanted to work with Ben but I was wondering if you would be willing to work with Jen and Gavin? I think your organization skills, Jen's Art skills, and Gavin's Python skills could make a power team!" Most students will be amiable and you get lots of buy-in from students for minimal work.

Immediately before they complete the index cards, guide them through a quick reflection process where they, in writing, write privately about what they want out of a partner and what they don't want out of a partner. Even a bulleted list works for this. It helps put them in a reflective frame of mind to make more informed decisions.

If it works for the context of the project, you can also add competency preferences to the index card, but things start to get pretty complicated.

Grouping by ability or engagement level is a highly controversial topic. On one hand, students deserve to work with peers of similar ability. On the other hand, robbing a group of diversity removes tremendous growth opportunities for all involved. This topic warrants its own book!

It helps if students have a defined route to vent frustrations and to ask you for help with group dynamics. This could be an index card they submit every Friday, an email they send you, a one-on-one student check-in, or anything else that feels natural.

Have students write their own name one side of the index card, and the rest of the information on the other so that, as a teacher, you don't bring your own bias' into the equation. Then you can flip them over, see what groups were formed, and make adjustments if needed.

Method 2 - Say Wha...!?

This is a method that can be quite useful for shorter term groupings but may be seen as cavalier for long term projects.

As students come into the class, ask them to arrange themselves by something trivial but concrete (height, age, shirt color, etc.), with no context as to why.

Once they arrange themselves, quickly count them off into groups as you walk down the line and (on the fly) make some flash decisions about who to put where if you notice a pairing you don't like. Before they know what's happening, they'll be in groups and it'll be done.

This method works well because it happens so quickly that anxieties aren't given time to rise and student politics don't interfere. It just feels like something that happened as opposed to a deliberate slight or tension. There are, however, a few things to consider with this method:

If students start to predict outcomes and strategize, mix-up your process. Instead of selecting in groups

STRATEGIES TO FORM TEAMS

from left to right, start from the outside and work your way to the middle.

Be cautious with your selection schemes and methods. By selecting for something as simple as eye color you can accidentally group your class by race, or accidentally group your class by gender by filtering for height.

Mind-Benders:

If you've read this far then you're a serious PBL educator and I want to hit you with a few more mind-benders and considerations:

Groups are normally selected at the very beginning of a project. Sometimes it makes more sense for students to work to a certain point individually, only then grouping up for a final culmination. This helps to guarantee base-level competence across the board and lends to wiser group choices.

A PBL classroom has a tendency to favor the extrovert but class discussions, solo vs. group time, and written vs. oral work helps to balance the environment for introverts.

Despite your best efforts, groups will not be perfect. Just do your best and embrace the humanity of it. When conflicts arise, take the time to work it out with students, develop their Social-Emotional Learning Skills, and if it comes down to it...sometimes it's even OK to move kids between groups mid-project.

Real life is messy.

SECONDARY TEAM CONTRACT

TEAM AGREEMENT

COMMUNICATION

What are our norms for discussion and communication?

How will we collaborate when we are not meeting in person?
E.g. File sharing, real-time collaboration, project management system, etc.

How will we conduct team meetings? How often?

How will we make decisions? How will we resolve conflict?

Just like in the adult world, team members can be fired during a project. What would justify a firing?
What steps would be taken prior to a firing?

ROLES & RESPONSIBILITIES

Which roles will team members take on? What responsibilities will they have?
What are they the best fit for this role? What strengths do they bring?

How will your team support team members when they have excused or unexcused absences?

SECONDARY TEAM CONTRACT

TEAM AGREEMENT			
TASKS & MILESTONES			
TASKS & MILESTONES	DUE DATE	LEAD	TASK STATUS

ADDITIONAL AGREEMENTS

TEAM SIGNATURES	

UPPER ELEMENTARY TEAM CONTRACT

TEAM AGREEMENT

Team Name: _____   Project: _____

BEING A TEAM MEMBER

| My name is _____ and I will help with the project by... | My name is _____ and I will help with the project by... | My name is _____ and I will help with the project by... |

TALKING AS A TEAM

| When we speak to each other, we... | When we make decisions, we... | Also, we... |

WORKING AS A TEAM

| When we don't agree, we... | If someone misses something, we will... | We will meet on... |

LOWER ELEMENTARY TEAM CONTRACT

TEAM AGREEMENT

Team Name: _____   Project: _____

BEING A TEAM MEMBER

My name is _____
and I will help with the project by...

My name is _____
and I will help with the project by...

My name is _____
and I will help with the project by...

TALKING AS A TEAM

When we speak to each other, we...

When we speak to each other, we...

WORKING AS A TEAM

When we don't agree, we...

If someone misses something, we will...

INDIVIDUAL COLLABORATION JOURNAL

COLLABORATION – INDIVIDUAL PERFORMANCE

As you move through the phases of design, consider your role as a team member. Review the collaboration rubric for Individual Performance. Set some goals for yourself to guide your work within your team.

	TAKES RESPONSIBILITY FOR ONESELF	HELPS THE TEAM	RESPECTS OTHERS
Check-in #1: **Set at least one goal for each strand.** Consider using the SMART goal framework to ensure your goals are specific, measureable, attainable, realistic and timely.			
Check-in #2: **Review progress with your goals.** How have you met your goals? Have you exceeded them? How so?			
Check-in #3: **Reflect on your individual performance.** Where are you strong in each category? Where do you have room to improve in each category? How did your team role affect your collaboration? Any surprises?			

TEAM COLLABORATION JOURNAL

COLLABORATION – TEAM PERFORMANCE

As you move through the project, consider…

1. your role as a team member and
2. your team as an organism.

Review your team agreement document and think about your team work so far.

Check-in #1:

Review your team agreement. Have you followed everything?

If so, how well?
If not, why not?

Were any unnecessary?

Check-in #2:

Have any agreements fallen by the wayside?

Do they need to be completed, or are they unnecessary to your team's success?

If yes, who should take the lead?

Check-in #3:

How did your team agreement help you succeed as a team?

Were their challenges? How would you use a team agreement differently to prevent, or better address, future challenges?

RECOMMENDED READINGS & RESOURCES

BOOKS

Tool Time for Education Handbook
http://www.langfordlearning.com/
This is a big, colorful book of protocols that can be used for just about anything. The book is intended to be used by educators in adult contexts, though many of these protocols could and should be taught to students, with adaptations as needed.

The Five Dysfunctions of Team by Patrick Lencioni. This book is intended for business professionals, but it is absolutely relevant to teachers in classrooms as well. It addresses key elements vital to building strong teams and is a quick and enjoyable read.

ARTICLES & BLOGS

Using Conflict Resolution Speak: Learn more at: https://www.responsiveclassroom.org/article/conflict-resolution-protocol-elementary-classrooms

Using Giraffe Language for Conflict Resolution: Learn more at: http://positivesharing.com/2006/07/5-essential-steps-to-resolve-a-conflict-at-work/

Nurturing Collaboration: 5 Strategies
https://www.edutopia.org/blog/nurturing-collaboration-5-strategies-joshua-block

WEBSITES

The 5 Love Languages for Kids. Use This Free, Quick Profile Assessment for Youngsters at: http://www.5lovelanguages.com/profile/children/

National School Reform Faculty Protocols
Hundreds of protocols created for teachers, by teachers. Most are freely available online: http://www.nsrfharmony.org/free-resources/protocols

Edutopia.org
Most of their section on social and emotional learning is relevant to collaboration.

REFLECT & CONNECT	
Why bother teaching collaboration? What is it exactly?	
What have you learned about how to teach collaboration? About assessing collaboration?	
How would you use the resources for collaboration in your own practice?	
Respond to this key question from your perspective as a teacher: How can I teach and assess collaboration skills?	

WHY, WHAT & HOW?

What is creativity and what is innovation? The terms creativity and innovation are thrown around a lot. Their meaning can feel nebulous at times. What are they exactly? Why do we always hear them paired together? Indeed these two skills are linked in important ways.

> " Creativity is the process of having original ideas that have value. "
> -Sir Ken Robinson (2010)

Creativity, as defined by Sir Ken Robinson, requires nothing more than generating ideas. You don't have to do anything with them. They can live in your head.

Innovation, on the other hand, asks us to take our ideas to fruition. Innovation requires that we manifest our ideas into reality. Innovation results in tangible novelty.

> " Innovation is the creation of something new and useful. "
> -Linda Hill (2014)

This is why we so often see creativity and innovation paired as important partners in crime. Creativity is about ideation and innovation is about production.

Linda Hill dives deeper in her 2014 TED Talk on Managing Collective Creativity. She breaks creativity and innovation into three important skill sets that work together to achieve successful outcomes. They are: (1) Creative Agility, (2) Creative Abrasion and (3) Creative Resolution.

CREATIVE AGILITY: This is about fluency with generating ideas - both in large quantities and that often defy convention.

CREATIVE ABRASION: This is about discussing, judging, debating, advocating for and selecting the best ideas.

CREATIVE RESOLUTION: This is about taking the best ideas from concept to refined reality.

Creativity, as defined by Sir Ken Robinson, is the essence of Creative Agility. On the other hand, think about Creative Resolution as innovation - the tangible production of ideas. Creative Abrasion becomes an important step between Creative Agility and Creative Resolution in which we determine which ideas, conceptually and in development, are worth pursuing and how to do that. Abrasion is also about revising, refining and improving along the way.

Creativity and innovation must be taught, practiced and developed. It is not a question of being good at them or not being good at them, at an inborn level. Creative Agility, Abrasion and Resolution can be unpacked into sets of behaviors that can be explicitly taught, practiced and refined. Furthermore, some of the behaviors require interactions that can be optimized through facilitation of structures and protocols.

In addition, the quality of the environment can enable or disable the targeted sets of behaviors. Therefore, creativity and innovation can be both implicitly encouraged by the environment and explicitly taught and practiced with the help of the teacher in the context of schools.

Finding the sweet spot for creativity and innovation in schools requires that teachers are modeling behaviors that teach, elicit and facilitate student behaviors, all of which are enabled by learning spaces conducive to creative and innovative work. For more information on these specific sets of behaviors, see the resources for assessing creativity and innovation.

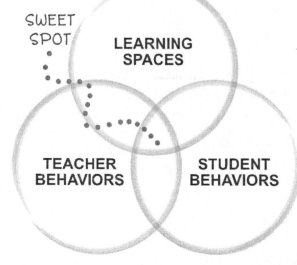

SWEET SPOT

LEARNING SPACES

TEACHER BEHAVIORS

STUDENT BEHAVIORS

The Creativity & Innovation Ecosystem - You are not alone in this work. A whole ecosystem has formed around creativity and innovation called The Maker Movement: A growing network of DIYers - inventors, designers, artisans and tinkerers - focused on production over consumption.

> **MAKERSPACE:** "...creative, DIY spaces where people can gather to create, invent, and learn. In libraries they often have 3D printers, software, electronics, craft and hardware supplies and tools, and more...sometimes also referred to as hackerspaces, hackspaces, and fablabs " (Kroski, 2013).

People and organizations are participating at all levels - from individuals in their garages to self-organizing groups converging together to share spaces, tools and ideas in MakerSpaces that a free to anyone, at libraries and communities centers, at paid membership-based facilities and more.

There are impromptu Maker communities to large-scale participation in organized MakerFaires. Schools and small communities can and do even host their own mini Maker Faires.

Schools have embraced the Maker Movement as well and are transitioning libraries to learning commons and MakerSpaces in which learning can shift from a consumption-focused activity to a production-focused activity.

> **MAKER FAIRE:** "an all-ages gathering of tech enthusiasts, crafters, educators, tinkerers, hobbyists, engineers, science clubs, authors, artists, students, and commercial exhibitors. All of these 'makers' come to Maker Faire to show what they have made and to share what they have learned." ("Maker Faire", 2016).

The Maker Movement extends into industry where well-established companies, like Google, Pixar and more have created spaces that foster collaboration and flexible creativity and innovation because they recognize that "space transmits culture (Doorley, 2014) and that "the environment influences human behavior."

> " Space transmits culture. "
> -Doorley & Wittholf, (2014)
> Authors of Make Space

> " The environment influences human behavior. "
> -Frederik Pferdt,
> Global Program Manager for
> Creativity and Innovation
> at Google

If they want to build a culture that fosters creative and innovative mindsets, than they know they must create spaces that promote creative and innovative behaviors. Notably, Google created "Google Garage" to optimize the use of their 20% time structures, in which employees can use 20% of their working hours to pursue projects of their choosing, based on their interests and passions. This structure was the famous inspiration for the Genius Hour movement in K-12 schools.

Higher education has embraced the Maker Movement and MakerSpaces as well, with Stanford's famous dSchool, Harvard's Innovation Lab and MIT's Fab Lab and many more sweeping the globe.

The Maker Movement is more about mindsets than about stuff. Maker Mindsets are Hacker Mindsets, in which we attempt to find clever and simple solutions to everyday problems, both big and small.

If you're wondering how all of this will help prepare students of today for their post-secondary lives of tomorrow, don't worry, it will! The Maker Mindset has increasingly become way of the world in individual's lives, in communities, in higher education, in entrepreneurship and in industry. Students who adopt this mindset have the potential to become agents of positive change in the world around them. They can become producers in a sea of consumers. And let's not forget that thinking and working in this way can be fun, fulfilling, connected and often even positively impactful to the ever-changing world around us.

> " Being a maker is about not taking the world as it's given. "
> -Yang (2013)

TEACHING BRAINSTORMING METHODS

100 IDEAS IN 10 MINUTES

Use this approach when there are a lot of participants and you're still early in the process. This works best when there are still tons of directions and possibilities for solutions.

Pssst...
Want to try some of these? But, maybe feeling out of your comfort zone? That's ok, just start by starting.

TRY IT

Name a few scribes who can take down 10-20 ideas each on separate sheets of chart paper or sections of a white board. Set a timer for ten minutes. The group calls out ideas and the scribes call back the idea they are going to write down to avoid duplicates. Ten minutes later, you can have 100+ ideas.

PICK ONE...OR TWO...

THREE METHODS TO GET STARTED

WORD LISTING

Get out your trusty thesaurus

Free association of words related to and contrary to your idea can help generate new and useful ideas and extensions to your ideas.

STEP 1

Create three columns on a white board, a piece of chart paper or even just a simple sheet of paper. In the first column, write the prompt, question, problem or key area of focus for your project or challenge. Then write words, ideas and concepts that are related to your prompt.

STEP 2

Review what you wrote in the first column and select the word, idea or concept that resonates with you the most. Place what resonated with you at the top of the second column and then think of words, ideas and concepts related to that, and list them in the second column.

STEP 3

The third column is "opposites world" in which you'll list words, concepts and ideas that are the opposite of what you wrote in the first column. Think about antonyms, opposites and contradictions. Sometimes this gets zany, which can be fun!

STEP 4

Look for and visually connect patterns and relationships between all three columns. You're looking for that "ah ha" moment now!

4 PHASES

Use the 4 phases in order, beginning with (1) fluency, then (2) flexibility, then (3) originality & finally end with (4) elaboration on the best ideas.

Time constraints can actually increase the flow of ideas. As in 2-5 minutes per phase.

1 - 2 - 3 - 4

CREATIVE AGILITY RESOURCES

TEACHING BRAINSTORMING METHODS

YES, AND . . . .

Also known as "plussing" This is based golden rule of improv...where you must accept what someone offers you and build off of it.

STEP 1

Form a circle with a group of about 4-16 participants. Then, name the prompt, challenge or problem to be addressed. Allow for what may feel like a period of awkward silence until the first person in the group names a possible solution or idea.

STEP 2

Now, proceed clockwise around the circle to build on the first idea by saying, "yes, and..." Essentially, you are "plussing" the idea. Continue to develop the idea in this manner until the ideation momentum dies out. Go with what you have or do another round until you feel you can move forward in the project process.

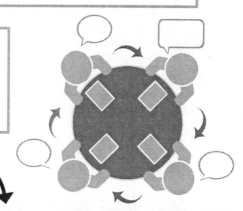

FOUR METHODS TO DEVELOP EARLY IDEAS

FUTURE THINKING

Future thinking is all about challenging the conventions in our present world. Start this type of brainstorming with a semi-developed idea/design in mind. Then, flash forward one year, two years, ten years to imagine how the idea/design could be improved in the absence of the constraints of our present day lives and world.

COMIC STRIPS

This brainstorming technique is based on the game Mad Libs.

Create a quick Mad Lib frame that is relevant to your semi-developed idea/design. Include lots of blanks.

TRY IT

E.g. The _____ reminds me of _____ and _____ because _____.

Do the same frame multiple times, or let other people give it a try after hearing about your idea/design.

Try to tease out some patterns. This can be a fun prompt to use in a focus group.

ROLE PLAYING

Role playing as an approach to brainstorming is exactly what it sounds like. Get two or more people together to act out how a semi-developed idea/design would be discussed, used and/or experienced by a potential user.

TRY IT

During the role play, think about the behaviors, feelings, questions, pain points and more that participants are experiencing. Does this give you ideas for how you could revise your idea/design? This approach is particularly useful when you are developing services.

33

TEACHING BRAINSTORMING METHODS

STEP 1
Generate an umbrella term that captures the essence of your overall challenge or project.

STEP 2
Now, jot down the first thing - one word, idea, concept, adjective or item - that comes to mind when you think about that umbrella term.

STEP 3
Now consider the umbrella term and the new word together. Engage in free association to attempt to generate new connections, patterns or ideas

STEP 4
Rinse and repeat until, hopefully, you achieve a breakthrough!

BRUTETHINK
Ever get stuck in a creative process?

Use this technique to help get "unstuck."

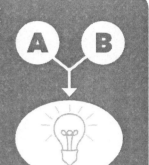

Pssst...
You know the drill.
Jot down your faves below.
Try tagging a student to lead one...

TWO METHODS FOR WHEN YOU'RE STUCK

IDEA INVERSION

OPPOSITES
WORLD

Try flipping your idea on its head...

Though seemingly counter-intuitive, sometimes the best breakthroughs happen when you think of the opposites of your target.

WHAT WILL YOU TRY?

TRY IT

Like with the word listing method, this approach requires spending some time in opposites world. Consider an idea or concept that isn't working well, or perhaps take the problem that your project or design challenge is attempting to solve. Now, think about achieving the exact opposite of the goal. Elaborate all the possible variations of the opposite by listing words, adjectives, protocols, procedures, concepts and steps that would foster the opposite. Sometimes, in doing this we identify the necessary mechanisms to achieve the opposite. If we flip that, we can sometimes breakthrough on how to achieve the actual target.

TEACHING BRAINSTORMING METHODS

MIND MAPPING

A visual method of brainstorming that helps individuals or groups name and connect a variety of diverse ideas and concepts to find trends and patterns.

prompt

STEP 1

To begin this visual brainstorming process, write the prompt, question, problem or key focus in the center of a white board, a piece of chart paper or even just a simple sheet of paper.

STEP 2

Jot down words, concepts, ideas and more in a way that connects them to the central prompt and that connects them to one another. If you run out of ideas, try creating a section that lists words, concepts and ideas that are the opposite of your area of focus.

STEP 3

Continue to freely build out the various extensions from the original prompt by naming related words, concepts and ideas.

STEP 4

Review the range of ideas, look for trends and patterns in order to gather and build on the best ideas.

THREE VISUAL BRAINSTORMING METHODS

COMIC STRIPS

This approach to brainstorming is all about empathizing with the user experience.

By simply imagining how users would view and use a product, concept or service we can gain insight on how to advance the idea.

STEP 1

Get started by sketching a user or scene of users in a cartoon-like format with speech bubbles. Capture potential environment and activities that would be going on. Can't sketch well? You can use a printed pictures instead.

STEP 2

Now, imagine and include dialog to what is now a storyboard in a way that mirrors the potential user experience. It may look like a comic strip.

STEP 3

What can you learn from the story to improve your idea? Keep referencing this comic strip during your design project. You can change the dialog, as needed.

PICTURE ASSOCIATION

This method of visual brainstorming relies on pictures and other visual materials as a source of inspiration for generating new and useful ideas.

STEP 1

Getting started with this method requires a bit of homework. You'll need to print out a variety of pictures - they can be photos, sketches, graphics and illustrations. They should be related to your challenge or project. You can get materials for web searches, books, magazines and more.

STEP 2

Now organize all of the materials you printed into like-groupings. How are they related? Name each grouping to capture the interconnectedness. These groups can be remixed and renamed numerous times in an effort to find new patterns and categories of likeness.

STEP 3

Use the process until you feel inspired to run with an idea for your challenge.

ASSOCIATING SYMBOLICALLY

Represent a concept or idea using another representation, similar to analogies. Leads students to be able to associate, one of the essentials in creative thinking. It also helps them develop abstract thinking. Examples:

- How are the three branches of government like a computer? Like a cheeseburger?

- Make tacos by using the distributive property.

- Dance the process of the water cycle

SUBSTITUTING

Substitute different items, theories, concepts, or ideas for common uses. This helps students develop the capacity to recognize patterns and make connections that might otherwise go unnoticed. Examples:

- Explain how Newton's First Law of Motion applies to character development

- If we substitute FDR for Lincoln as president during the Civil War, how might he have handled things differently?

- If you're right handed, use your left hand to paint or sculpt or vice-versa.

- Use Legos to construct 3D bar graphs
- Also See SCAMPER (*pg. 33*)

QUESTIONING

Explicitly teach types of questions, levels of questions and questioning strategies, such as:

- Convergent vs. divergent

- Factual questions: What are the parts of a cell? When did the French Revolution take place?

- Conceptual questions: How do we define sustainability? Why is it structured like that?

- Procedural questions: How do we write a book review? Why did we get outcome A, when we should have gotten outcome B?

- What if? Questions: What if Truman had NOT dropped the bomb?

- Logistical questions: When is the exhibition?

TABLEAU

What it is: A group of people pose to recreate a scene, typically depicting an event. They hold still and do not speak. The audience is left to interpret what they see. This has wide applications to tap into student's creative juices while building abstract thinking. Ideas for Tableau:

- Illustrate a pivotal scene in a story

- Illustrate a concept such as symmetry, or illustrate a procedure like photosynthesis.

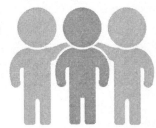

SOCRATIC SEMINAR

A strategy for text-based discussion and building background knowledge, this strategy helps us to build deeper understanding through text-based discussions and questioning. It can also be useful in teaching and practicing communication and discussion techniques, language and strategies. The two formats below represent how to physically structure the discussion. Multiple modifications are available.

SOCRATIC SMACKDOWN!

Socratic Smackdown was developed by the Institute of Play and is described by them as, "a versatile discussion-based humanities game to practice argumentation around any text or topic..." While they state that the game is designed for grades 6 through 12, many elementary teachers use it as well. They go on to say that , "it is a unique multi player game in which students learn how to discuss challenging topics while competing to earn points. Because earning points is done through using discussion strategies and language, it creates an opportunity to have fun, discuss an issue and practice how to discuss well. Materials and tutorials can be downloaded for free at the Institute for Play's Website.

FORMAT A : FISHBOWL

FORMAT B : PILOT & WINGMAN

PHILOSOPHICAL CHAIRS

This strategy helps students form a position on an issue. They decide if they agree or disagree with a statement (or they take a side on an issue.) Then they arrange themselves by position physically within a space. Both sides on the position discuss the issue. Students can change their position on an issue and physically move to the other section.

Rules: (1) One person speaks at a time. (2) The discussion. moves from Side A to Side B evenly. (3) Individuals may speak more than once, but they must let others on their side speak before contributing again. (4) If/when one changes position, they change sides physically. This can take place during the protocol.

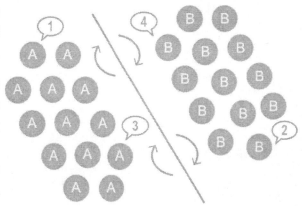

DESIGN THINKING AND THE ENGINEERING DESIGN CYCLE

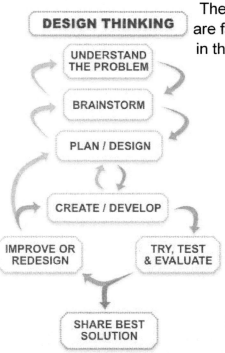

DESIGN THINKING

- UNDERSTAND THE PROBLEM
- BRAINSTORM
- PLAN / DESIGN
- CREATE / DEVELOP
- IMPROVE OR REDESIGN
- TRY, TEST & EVALUATE
- SHARE BEST SOLUTION

These two methods of inquiry are fairly similar. They are used in the adult world by designers and by engineers to conceptualize, plan, create and improve new "things" that have value.

Increasingly, teachers, students and schools at all levels are using these methods, which are already common in industry, to frame a process for making and creating.

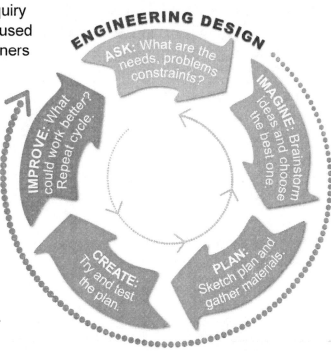

ENGINEERING DESIGN

- **ASK:** What are the needs, problems constraints?
- **IMAGINE:** Brainstorm ideas and choose the best one.
- **PLAN:** Sketch plan and gather materials.
- **CREATE:** Try and test the plan.
- **IMPROVE:** What could work better? Repeat cycle.

Generally speaking, the Engineering Design Cycle is used to create structures, systems, machines, engines & code. Design Thinking handles everything else.

SCAMPER

As a unifying strategy, try using this mneumonic device to confirm or improve the strength of an idea in progress or that is near completion.

S ubstitue something

C ombine it with something else

A dapt something to it

M odify or magnify it

P ut it to some other use

E liminate something

R eserve or rearrange it

MODELING

Teach students to use a variety of modeling tools to model systems, concepts or ideas. MIT experts say modeling is a new essential skill. Examples:

- Model zoo enclosure prototypes using Sketchup

- Create short story prewrites using FreeMind or BubbleUs

- Model a biome using Kodu

- Model number factors using Excel

CREATIVITY & INNOVATION RESOURCES
ASSESSING LEARNING SPACES

CREATIVITY & INNOVATION - LEARNING SPACES

PROMOTES INTERACTION / FOSTERS FLEXIBLE COLLABORATION	NEVER / NONE	SELDOM / SOME	SOMETIMES / MOST	FREQUENTLY / ALL

- Students are grouped in teams for the majority of work
- Open space is present and/or easily created to facilitate group movement activities
- Hierarchy is diminished by the absence of "power places"
  (e.g. the teacher's desk at the "front" of the room, or the "head" of a table)
- Large group and small group presentations are easily accommodated
- Digital space is available for collaborative discussions
- Time and structure are provided for quick feedback from peers and/or outside experts followed by iterating in close proximity

PHYSICALLY ADAPTABLE	NEVER / NONE	SELDOM / SOME	SOMETIMES / MOST	FREQUENTLY / ALL

- Furniture is easily reconfigured for the task at hand
- Space is purposefully adapted to the type of work to be done
- Space is available for ad hoc team meetings
- Teacher area/desk absent or placed in a non-prominent location; the majority of the room is student work-space
- Room maps (for various configurations) are available, but don't limit novel configurations

PROVIDES RICH ACCESS TO MATERIALS	NEVER / NONE	SELDOM / SOME	SOMETIMES / MOST	FREQUENTLY / ALL

- There is access to hardware such as, but not limited to: 3D printers, microcontrollers, laser cutters, welding machines, soldering irons, CAD, modeling software, MakeDo kits, duct tape, tools, spare parts, cardboard, plastic, metal, wire, gears and batteries
- Informational resources are available (books, pictures, old prototypes, or models)
- Many reference, idea and process visual aids and posters are present
- Digital space is available with resources related to idea generation, design and prototyping
- Video conferencing capabilities are available and promote access to virtual experts

BIASED TOWARD ACTION & PRODUCTION / ENABLES RAPID PROTOTYPING & ITERATION	NEVER / NONE	SELDOM / SOME	SOMETIMES / MOST	FREQUENTLY / ALL

- Time is viewed as a learning space resource
- Time is provided for students to pursue ideas of personal interest
- Writing surfaces are prevalent for group brainstorming, designing and/or planning
- Inexpensive prototyping materials are available
- Easy cleanup procedures, roles and tools maximize time for prototyping

NOTES

ASSESSING TEACHER BEHAVIORS

CREATIVITY & INNOVATION - TEACHER BEHAVIORS

GIVES PERMISSION TO QUESTION, TAKE RISKS AND INNOVATE	NEVER / NONE	SELDOM / SOME	SOMETIMES / MOST	FREQUENTLY / ALL

Frequently challenges students to ask questions, make proposals, and lead initiatives. Teaches students to interact with adults and bureaucracy appropriately. Guides students on how to adapt in the face of rejection.

MODELS CREATIVE & INNOVATIVE BEHAVIORS	NEVER / NONE	SELDOM / SOME	SOMETIMES / MOST	FREQUENTLY / ALL

Models:
• Observing and asking questions. May prompt students to ask higher quality questions (types of questions)
• Recognizing patterns & making connections between concepts, ideas, and situations (analogies, metaphors, associating)
• Considering multiple perspectives, using protocols like Socratic Seminar, Philosophical Chairs & Silent Debate
• Sharing and advocating for ideas, through social skills, active listening and use of discussion prompts/frames
• Taking appropriate risks (assessing potential impacts)
• Iterating and reframing failure (Design Thinking, the engineering design cycle, etc.)
• How to learn from others to produce original work that has value (how to recognize opportunities)

EXPLICITLY TEACHES:	NEVER / NONE	SELDOM / SOME	SOMETIMES / MOST	FREQUENTLY / ALL

Iterative Design Processes: Provides well planned as well as impromptu lessons, activities and modeling as well as by creating projects that require using iterative design processes, such as:
  • Design thinking   • The Engineering Design Cycle

Questioning: Provides well planned instruction on types of questions, levels of questions, question posing as well as organization and prioritization of questions.

Brainstorming: Provides well planned instruction and models the use of multiple methods of brainstorming. Reviews their scope of usefulness. Prompts students to think about which methods work best in different situations.

Associating: Provides frequent instruction and practice with analogies, symbolic association, analogies, visual representations and metaphors.

Substituting: Integrates frequent instruction and practice with substitution activities, such as asking "what if" questions as well as exploring opposites and contradictions.

Modeling: Using modeling tools, such as: CAD, gaming, Google Sketchup, mind-mapping and more.

FRAMES FREQUENT DESIGN CHALLENGES	NEVER / NONE	SELDOM / SOME	SOMETIMES / MOST	FREQUENTLY / ALL

Frames and integrates design challenges as the foundational framework of tasks. These design challenges may range in duration - from less than an hour to multi-month projects.

CONNECTS IDEAS, VIEWPOINTS, AND PEOPLE	NEVER / NONE	SELDOM / SOME	SOMETIMES / MOST	FREQUENTLY / ALL

Integrates protocols to structure a process to help students see connections between ideas, viewpoints and people as well as to facilitate a cross-pollination of ideas. Varies group composition and purposes, as needed.

NOTES

CREATIVITY AND INNOVATION - STUDENTS BEHAVIORS

OBSERVES AND ASKS QUESTIONS	NEVER / NONE	SELDOM / SOME	SOMETIMES / MOST	FREQUENTLY / ALL

- Frequently observes the world around them. Keeps an idea journal.
- To begin a project, develops 20-30 questions and/or need to knows to be addressed.
- Organizes & prioritizes questions, as needed:
  - Convergent vs. divergent
  - Factual questions: What are the parts of a cell? When did the French Revolution take place?
  - Conceptual questions: How do we define sustainability? Why is it structured like that?
  - Procedural questions: How do we write a book review? Why did I get outcome A, instead of outcome B?
  - What if? Questions: What if Truman had NOT dropped the bomb?
  - Logistical questions: When is the exhibition?
- Adds or adapts questions as research leads in new directions.
- Delegate who will answer which questions and how they be aggregated

SEES PATTERNS & MAKES CONNECTIONS	NEVER / NONE	SELDOM / SOME	SOMETIMES / MOST	FREQUENTLY / ALL

- Recognizes and articulates patterns in and across literature, informational texts, historical eras and movements, and/or scientific, mathematical and/or artistic principles.
- Sees and makes connections that lead to novel solutions to problems, or new understandings about concepts or ideas.
- Shares concepts and ideas using through alternative representations. Examples:
  - How are the three branches of government like a computer? Cheeseburger?
  - Making tacos by using the distributive property. • Dancing the process of the water cycle.
- Uses substitution to ask "what if?" questions. Examples: What if….
  - …the author changed this character to a male? Or removed the character completely?
  - …I substitute sand for charcoal in my water filter experiment?
  - …FDR were president during the Civil War? JFK during the Great Depression?
  - …Newton's Three Laws were applied to literature?

CONSIDERS MULTIPLE PERSPECTIVES	NEVER / NONE	SELDOM / SOME	SOMETIMES / MOST	FREQUENTLY / ALL

Seeks to understand first, before speaking. Uses active listening skills, empathy, and various types of questions to understand other perspectives. Articulates multiple perspectives while considering their place in the solution and/or new understanding.

SHARES AND ADVOCATES FOR IDEAS	NEVER / NONE	SELDOM / SOME	SOMETIMES / MOST	FREQUENTLY / ALL

Shares drafts, ideas, solutions, answers and perspectives throughout the process. Disagrees respectfully. Maintains an open-mind. Willing to shift opinions, when appropriate.

ITERATES & TAKES APPROPRIATE RISKS	NEVER / NONE	SELDOM / SOME	SOMETIMES / MOST	FREQUENTLY / ALL

Makes early attempts - not afraid to fail forward. Reflects on what doesn't work and why. Improves work in progress. Assesses the potential impacts of a decision or action.

USES MODELING TOOLS	NEVER / NONE	SELDOM / SOME	SOMETIMES / MOST	FREQUENTLY / ALL

Uses a variety of modeling tools as needed to model systems, concepts, or ideas. Examples:
- Model zoo enclosure prototypes using Sketchup
- Create short story prewrite using Freemind or BubbleUs
- Model a biome using Kodu
- Model number factors using Excel

PRODUCES ORIGINAL WORK THAT HAS VALUE	NEVER / NONE	SELDOM / SOME	SOMETIMES / MOST	FREQUENTLY / ALL

Learner is production-focused, with an emphasis on producing original products, performances, presentations and services that have an impact, provide value, are beneficial and are useful.

CREATIVITY & INNOVATION RESOURCES
GO DEEPER - RECOMMENDED CONTENT

BOOKS

Creating Innovators: The Making of Young People Who Will Change the World, Tony Wagner, 2012
This is a wonderful book with a lot of case studies about fostering creativity in our schools. He makes a compelling case for the fact that innovators are created, not born. Often, this is by teachers and schools who are breaking from convention.

The Maker Movement Manifesto: Rules for Innovation in the New World of Crafters, Hackers, and Tinkerers, by Mark Hatch, 2013.
The author provide background on the Maker Movement and creates a compelling call to action.

World Class Learners: Educating Creative and Entrepreneurial Students, Yong Zhao, 2012
Yong Zhao originally thought that China's educational system was better than ours, but after much research he discovered exactly the opposite. We do a better job of instilling the entrepreneurial spirit and creativity, but we do it by accident. He argues for a intentional approach to teaching these concepts.

Creative Workshop, David Sherwin
Full of design strategies and a multitude of design challenges that are quick and build creative agility.

Make Space, John Wiley & Sons, 2012
One of the coolest books about using space to support different kinds of thinking. Lots of practical ideas for room layout.

Bringing Innovation to School, Susie Boss
An anecdotal look into the successes and challenges of multiple schools and teachers who attempted to shift towards innovation.

Five Minds for the Future by Howard Gardner, 2009
Great sections on the synthesizing mind and the creating mind. Some good definitions and concepts to ponder.

ARTICLES & BLOGS

The Innovator's DNA by Dyer, Gregersen, and Christenson, 2009
This article from Harvard Business Review articulates what creative people do in common with one another.

Seven Strategies That Encourage Neural Branching, Cardichio and Field, 1997
Great article about strategies to promote more creative thinking.

VIDEOS

TED - A crash course in creativity, by Tina Seelig.

The Art of Teaching Entrepreneurship and Innovation, by Tina Seelig.

WEBSITES

Stanford's dSchool:
http://dschool.stanford.edu/

Coding for Kids
https://www.tynker.com/
https://code.org/

Maker Movement Central
http://makezine.com/
http://makerfaire.com/
http://www.instructables.com/

CREATIVITY - WHY, WHAT & HOW?

REFLECT & CONNECT

Why bother teaching creativity & innovation?

What are creativity and innovation exactly?

It enhances the ability to change the classroom experience from teacher-talks-at-student (consumption) to active engagement + participation by all, with teacher as partner

Creativity = ideas Innovation = turning ideas into "tangible novelty"

What have you learned about how to teach creativity and innovation?

About assessing them?

How would you use the resources for creativity and innovation in your own practice?

Respond to this key question from your perspective as a teacher:

How can I teach and assess creativity and innovation?

WHY, WHAT & HOW?

What is Critical Thinking? Out of the 4 Cs, Critical thinking is generally the most misunderstood. In working with teachers, I often ask, "how would you define critical thinking?" A common answer is that critical thinking is analogous to higher order thinking skills. Essentially the lower levels of Bloom's Taxonomy do not require critical thinking and the higher levels *are critical thinking.* In other words, if students engage in an analysis task or an application task, then they are inherently engaging in critical thinking. It is for this reason that teachers utilising Project Based Learning often say things like, "students are doing complex work in this project, so they will have to be critically thinking." Unfortunately, this is not the case. Critical thinking doesn't occur spontaneously when faced with complex tasks. Critical thinking is a meta-level skill which means that if I am not engaging intentionally in critical thought, then I'm probably not critically thinking at all. So, if critical thinking is not just engaging in higher order thinking tasks, then what is it?

> Critical thinking is the art of analyzing and evaluating thinking with a view to improving it.
> -The Foundation for Critical Thinking (2006)

The Foundation for Critical Thinking defines critical thinking as, "...the art of analyzing and evaluating thinking with a view to improving it." (2006) In other words, it's thinking about your thinking with the goal to *improve your thinking, to improve the quality of thought itself.* Thus, it's a meta-task, we must be actively thinking about the act of doing it with the goal of doing it better.

Critical Thinking Can Occur at Any Order of Thinking.

Let's go back to the idea of higher order thinking. As an example, I could engage in analysis, and that would be analysis, not necessarily critical thinking. But, if I worked to improve the quality of my analysis, then that could rise to the level of critical thinking. Let's imagine I were tackling a lower-order thinking skill, like remembering. This order of thinking could be conducted with or without critical thinking. In the absence of critical thinking, I could simply attempt to remember something. However, a critical thinker might ask, "what are the best ways to remember?" This might lead to the discovery of pneumonic devices, note taking strategies, visual representations and more. A critical thinker might also ask, "what information is the most important to remember versus simply reference?" This could lead to a thoughtful and insightful process of categorizing information based on the goals and purposes behind remembering that information in the first place. Perhaps, a critical thinker would ask, "what type of learner am I and therefore which strategies would work best to help me remember?" A visual learner might recognize the need to organize visually that which needs to be remembered in order to anchor it to memory. In this way, a critical thinker would engage intentionally in tasks and/or processes in order to remember more accurately, more effectively and more efficiently. They might even go deeper and ask, "did it work and how do I know?" Then, they could reflect on the quality of the process by looking at evidence as to whether or not and to what extent remembering actually occurred. From there, based on the evidence, they could either affirm their process of remembering or attempt to improve it for the future. We can and we should work to improve the quality of our thinking at lower orders and at higher orders of thought. At first, we might legitimately feel that all of this seems arduous, and somewhat redundant. Though, like scaffolds, some of these intentional, careful steps and questioning processes can be removed or reduced once these ways of thinking have become more automatic and processes have been refined. Then, they can be revisited **44** only as needed.

CREATE

EVALUATE

ANALYZE

APPLY

UNDERSTAND

REMEMBER

Adapted from Bloom's Taxonomy

How Do We Develop Critical Thinkers? Roland Case, former Executive Director of the Critical Thinking Consortium in Canada, elucidates the idea that the teaching of critical thinking ought not be an afterthought to teaching content knowledge, skills and understandings outlined in our standards and programs of study, but rather critical thinking should be seen as, "... a powerful method of teaching all other aspects of the curriculum - both content and skill." (p. 46, 2005). Case goes on to say that,

> "inviting students to think critically about subject matter is effective at promoting both understanding of the content and mastery of the skills. Students who passively receive information are far less likely to understand what they have heard or read about than are students who have critically scrutinized, interpreted, applied or tested this information. Rather than compete with the teaching of subject matter and other thinking skills, critical thinking supports their development." (p. 46).

In addition to this idea that approaching the teaching of content through critical thinking, he also advocates for the intentional development of what he calls the "intellectual tools" (p. 46). for critical thinking. These domains of capacity can lead to critical thinking practices to become developed and more automatic in any individual's life. They include the following: (1) Critical Thinking Vocabulary, (2) Habits of Mind, (3) Content Knowledge, (4) Criteria for Judgement and (5) Thinking Strategies. (p. 49-50). A teacher working with intention can absolutely develop student capacity in each of these five domains. You may have already drawn the early, and fair, conclusion that developing critical thinkers is much more complex, dynamic and nuanced than teaching any of the other 4 Cs. Critical thinking interweaves with everything we do and requires skill sets and capacities in a variety of domains. Though, much of the work we can do to build creativity and innovation skills overlap with critical thinking.

CRITICAL THINKING VOCABULARY

THINKING STRATEGIES

DOMAINS OF CAPACITY FOR CRITICAL THINKING

HABITS OF MIND

CRITERIA FOR JUDGEMENT

CONTENT KNOWLEDGE

Adapted from Case, 2005

(1) Critical Thinking Vocabulary: This involves building clarity around terms and academic language in addition to teaching some informal logic, such as informal fallacies. E.g. Straw Man, Ad hominem, Hasty Generalization, etc. It is already considered best practice to teach academic language and given the inclusion of qualifiers around logic and reason in most sets of standards and learning outcomes for language arts, not to mention its vital importance in science and other disciplines, teaching informal fallacies, and for that matter formal logic, already ties into teaching content, better.

(2) Habits of Mind: This draws on the work of Arthur Costa and is about developing dispositions regarding how we interact with the world around us both independently and interdependently.

(3) Content Knowledge: Notably, some are surprised to see content knowledge as a domain of capacity for critical thinking. Though Case eloquently states that, "thinking without content is vacuous and content acquired without thought is mindless and inert." (p. 47).

> "...thinking without content is vacuous and content acquired without thought is mindless and inert."
> -Roland Case (2005)

(4) Criteria for Judgement: This is about routinizing the practice of making decisions and judgements, based on criteria, not preferences.

(5) Thinking Strategies: This is about learning processes for approaching thinking, doing and creating. It directly relates to learning and practicing various methods of inquiry. (*See pages 64-67*).

SOCRATIC SEMINAR

SOCRATIC SEMINAR

In this protocol can be useful in promoting critical thinking by building capacity with habits of mind, to promote using criteria for judgement and to deepen content knowledge and understandings. Participants (often students) usually engage in some preparatory tasks – reading a text, watching a video, generating questions, considering questions, etc.

Then, participants engage in a discussion, or series of discussions, using the protocol as a structure. The purpose of the discussion is primarily to seek to understand the targeted issue, concept or question more deeply, using new learning and information derived from evidence from texts or other media. Secondarily, it is also to share thinking, pose questions and consider others' perspectives. Furthermore, the protocol becomes a framework for actually teaching, practicing and reflecting on the use of discussion skills and language for discussion.

There are multiple formats that can be used to structure the discussion. The Pilot and Wingman format modifies the traditional format of Socratic Seminars to allow for greater movement, designation of roles and participation in discussion as well as active listening. Fishbowl and the use of a "hot seat" is another format for structuring the discussions in a Socratic Seminar.

The following sets of tools and resources can be used with students.

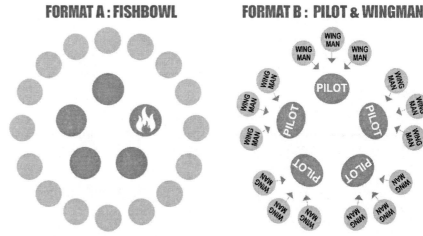

FORMAT A : FISHBOWL

FORMAT B : PILOT & WINGMAN

NORMS

- Listen carefully
- Address one another respectfully
- Base any opinions on the text
- Be tough on content, soft on people
- Address comments to the group (no side conversations)
- Use sensitivity to take turns and not interrupt others
- Monitor 'air time' - be concise when you share
- Be courageous in presenting your own thoughts and reasoning, but be flexible and willing to change your mind in the face of new and compelling evidence

SOCRATIC SEMINAR

DISCUSSION OBSERVATION & FEEDBACK TOOL

PARTICIPATION

Record a check for each time the discussion participant you are observing contributes to the discussion in a meaningful way

☐ ☐ ☐ ☐

☐ ☐ ☐ ☐

☐ ☐ ☐ ☐

ANALYSIS & REASONING

☐ Cite reasons and evidence for his/ her statements with support from the text
☐ Demonstrate that they had given thoughtful consideration to the topic
☐ Provide relevant comments
☐ Demonstrate organized thinking
☐ Move the discussion to a deeper level
☐ Other:

DISCUSSION SKILLS

☐ Speak loudly and clearly
☐ Stay on topic
☐ Talk to and make eye contact directly with other participants, rather than the teacher
☐ Stay focused on the discussion
☐ Invite other people into the discussion
☐ Share air time equally with others (didn't talk more than was fair to others)
☐ Other:

CIVILITY

☐ Listen to others attentively and respectfully
☐ Add to the discussion in a polite manner
☐ Avoid inappropriate language (slang, swearing)
☐ Maintain constructive exchanges
☐ Question others in a civil manner
☐ Disagree respectfully
☐ Other:

POST-DISCUSSION QUESTIONS FOR REFLECTION

What did like about the protocol?

What would you change about the protocol?

Would you use the protocol again? How?

Other:

CRITICAL THINKING RESOURCES
SOCRATIC SEMINAR

DISCUSSION SENTENCE STARTERS

REFERENCING THE TEXT	AGREEING
The section titled _____ is about...	I like the idea that...
The main idea of the passage...	I agree, the author...
In section ___ we learn...	Your point is well taken...
In paragraph ___, the author...	True, we should consider...
This (page or paragraph) is about...	I also found...
The author's central claim...	The author also states in paragraph ___ that...
The main point of the text is...	I had a similar experience...
A central point in the text is...	We should all consider...

REFERENCING THE TEXT	DISAGREEING
The graph illustrates...	Let's take a closer look at...
From the diagram we learn that...	My interpretation (or reading) of the passage...
The table compares...	Although I tend to agree, I think...
Based on the data, it is reasonable to conclude...	I hear what everyone is saying, but...
The image shows...	We might be misreading the author...
The table suggests...	I don't know if I agree...
The illustration provides...	Have we explored all angles...
	I respectfully disagree with the idea....

48

Good Reading Protocols (handwritten)

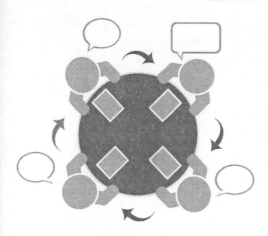

...this protocol, individuals read a text and "say something" to ...are their thinking, warms, cools, connections and questions about the text. To get started, simply divide the text into relatively equal sections. How many sections? It depends on the length of the text, though generally, each section should take an average of 3-7 minutes to read. Once the text is divided into sections, each individual silently and individual reads the first section of the text. While reading, individuals quietly note a few passages that are meaningful to them. Then, after everyone has finished reading, the facilitator starts a timer for 60 seconds for each individual, as they "say something." Their "say something" contribution must start with a quote from the text, then they may elaborate, share connections and more. There is no cross-talk, interruptions, discussions or responding to those who already said something. Highlighting multiple passages is important because if someone cites a passage another planned to cite, they must choose a different passage about which to "say something." Once everyone has said something about the first passage, everyone then silently reads the next passage. Then, each person is given 60 seconds to "say something" about the second passage. And so on, and so forth, until each section of the article has been read and everyone has said something. Benefits of this protocol include: (1) Splitting the article into short sections reduces "wait-time" typical of in-class readings, due to variations in individuals' reading speeds, (2) the chunking of the article allows for better processing of the content, (3) hearing others' contributions allows readers to get more from the article than they would have on their own, (4) prohibiting cross-talk promotes development of active listening skills and more.

PLUSES, MINUSES & QUESTIONS OF A TEXT

Individuals read an article and, with a pen, pencil or highlighter, they annotate the article with symbols for their "pluses" (+), which represent warms, positives, agreements and what they like about the text. They also indicate "minuses" (-), which represent cools, disagreements, negatives and what they dislike about the text. Lastly, they note "questions" (?), regarding elements they don't understand, want to consider further or aren't sure about. Once each individual has annotated the selected article with pluses, minuses and questions, they form small groups of 2-5 and discuss their pluses, minuses and questions, for 2-4 minutes each.

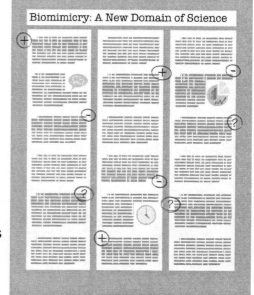

Biomimicry: A New Domain of Science

CRITICAL THINKING JOURNAL

Write the Focusing Question	
What is your preliminary understanding of the Focusing Question?	
Who is the affected in answering the Focusing Question? E.g. audience, users, stakeholders? What are their wants and/or needs?	
What do you need to know more about to answer the Focusing Question?	

CRITICAL THINKING JOURNAL

NEED TO KNOW (What do I need to know to answer the Focusing Question?)	NEW INFORMATION (What relevant information have I found or learned?)	SOURCE (Where did that information come from?)	CREDIBILITY (How do I know the information is accurate and/or credible? To what extent is it factual and/or biased?)

CRITICAL THINKING JOURNAL

MOST PROMISING IDEAS / SOLUTIONS / PROTOTYPES	HOW THEY COULD ACHIEVE CRITERIA?	HOW THEY COULD BE IMPROVED AND OR REVISED TO BETTER ACHIEVE CRITERIA?

CRITICAL THINKING JOURNAL

How could you best present your response to the Focusing Question?	
How could you justify your response with evidence & criteria?	
What were your limitations to answering the Focusing Question? What other perspectives should be considered? What implications for future work should be noted?	
What new understandings did you gain from the project? How could they transfer to other situations?	

REFLECT & CONNECT

CRITICAL THINKING - WHY, WHAT & HOW?

REFLECT & CONNECT

Why bother teaching critical thinking?

What is it exactly?

What have you learned about how to teach critical thinking?

About assessing it?

How would you use the resources for critical thinking in your own practice?

Respond to this key question from your perspective as a teacher:

How can I teach and assess critical thinking skills?

PRESENTATION AT A GLANCE
WHY, WHAT & HOW?

Why Learn to Present? Out of the 4 Cs, presentation is the most straightforward. The skills involved with both creating and delivering a high quality presentation can be taught, discovered, practiced and mastered. While I don't believe everyone needs to learn to become a world-class presenter, I do believe that in any field, discipline or context, being able to effectively communicate a message to those to whom the message matters or is simply interesting, is a valuable skill indeed. This can be true in both our personal and professional lives. The basic idea that we all have and will have "messages" to convey in our lives and developing presentation skills is about learning how to develop the best "medium" for our messages.

MESSAGE   MEDIUM

What About Fear Of Public Speaking? Jerry Seinfeld once joked that for most people, the fear of public speaking ranks higher than the fear of death. A few years ago, I met an young professional in Manhattan who worked for Goldman Sachs. His job was to teach executives how to give better presentations, because the company was tired of sitting through boring and ugly presentations. I asked him, "so, what is the secret to great presentations?" He replied quickly and simply: "practice." We get comfortable with presenting by practicing, we get over fears by practicing, we get good at techniques, by practicing them.

Karen Cheng is an amazing individual who loves learning new things, as an adult. While she's a software engineer by training, she likes to take on new "learning projects." Basically, she like to tackle learning random skill sets that interest her - card tricks, playing the guitar, juggling, dancing, etc. A few years ago, she became interested in learning how to dance. She started a 365-day project in which she practiced dancing, every single day. She videotaped herself each day, posted the videos to YouTube and then at the end created a time lapse video that shows her progress over the course of the year.

She reflected on her progress in an interview stating, "from day-to-day, I didn't really see any improvement, and that can be discouraging. But when you look back, first you'll cringe at how bad you were before, but then you'll feel good because of how far you came." She encourages others to tackle new skill sets and reminds us all that, "it is that fear of failure that keeps people from wanting to start, but if you admit to yourself that: 'hey, I could fail, what matters is that I tried,' you'd be surprised at what you could do." (Cheng, 2013). This is true with presentations skills as well. The only failure would be a failure to try.

> ❝ It is that fear of failure that keeps people from wanting to start, but if you admit to yourself that: 'hey, I could fail, what matters is that I tried,' you'd be surprised at what you could do. ❞
>
> -Karen Cheng (2013)

My Own Personal Journey With Presenting. As an individual with expertise in education, I am now asked to give presentations all over the world to teachers and leaders in schools and districts, at educational consortia as well as at gatherings for educators such as conferences, symposiums, seminars and more. After giving hundreds of presentations, I now feel very confident, even fearless, when giving presentations to small or large groups. This was not always true.

The first time I had to give a presentation in front of other people was when I was in tenth grade. Prior to starting tenth grade, instead of registering for the conventional English I course, I opted to register for Rhetoric. Why? No strong reason, Rhetoric sounded cooler. It turns out this Rhetoric course was the breeding grounds for the school's Speech and Debate team. And yes, the teacher for the Rhetoric class was also the Coach for the Speech and Debate team. My fellow classmates and I quickly discovered that we would be giving a lot of presentations, learning about oral communication techniques, styles and formats in addition to the history of Rhetoric.

The course was fascinating. After only a couple of weeks, I was given my first presentation assignment. This was mortifying, as I had never presented before, in my life. The parameters of the presentation assignment were based on a Speech and Debate event called "extemp." Extemp is short for extemporaneous speaking. In this speech event, competitors - known as "extempers" are given three prompts relating to the latest current events around the globe. From the moment they are handed the three prompts, a clock starts, and extempers then have only thirty minutes to prepare and rehearse a persuasive speech that should last no more than six minutes, on one of the three prompts. Over the course of thirty very quick minutes, they prepare speeches in a quiet, supervised space. Access to computers, and now Smartphones and other devices, is prohibited. The idea is that extempers must become well-versed on current events.

Of course, a key element of any strong persuasive argument, written or spoken, is the use of relevant and credible evidence. So, without access to computers, how do extempers access a bank of evidence to support their arguments? The common practice for extempers was to read the news from a variety of sources on a regular basis and then to organize "clippings" for all of these articles into an "extemp box" - actually a portable plastic file box. Extemp boxes are full of folders, that are full of all of these clippings, that are organized by current event. Extempers bring their extemp box, or boxes (sometimes with moving dollies) to be able to reference all of these sources during their thirty minute prep window.

Back to the clock starting - thirty minutes start ticking away and preparations begin. First, quickly weight the merits of each prompt. Then, pick one. Next, formulate a position on the prompt with an engaging introduction and conclusion. Now, craft typically three contentions to support the position. Then, bolster each contention with at least three sources. Oh, and did I mention that notes are strictly prohibited during the six minute presentation? True story. So, in addition to crafting and remembering the structure of their presentation, they must accurately memorize ALL the quotes AND respective sources. In short, a tiny bit of an extemp presentation, delivered entirely from memory, might sound like this:

> "...and now onto my second contention "..." This position was supported by Malcolm Gladwell in his New Yorker essay, entitled, "...." and published in November of 2008, in which he states, "..."

Extemp is hard. And there I was, a tenth grader, faced with giving an extemp speech as my first presentation in my life. No pressure. Granted, for this first try, my teacher modified the time constraints. I had overnight to do research and prepare. The next day in class, I gave my first ever presentation in front of my peers, and it was absolutely horrible. Throughout the entire presentation, I stared at the same spot on the carpet, and proceeded to hastily recite a poorly memorized speech.

Flash forward one year, and I was a state champion in extemporaneous speaking and a nationally qualified competitor. Flash forward into my adult life, and I am now an internationally recognized public speaker, who, ironically, speaks about the importance of teaching presentation skills! I, myself, learned those skills in high school. All because a teacher taught us. I wasn't inherently talented with presentation. My peers in class developed capacity with presentation right alongside me. Over the years, I've continued to grow and am still learning and improving the craft of communicating messages, with engaging mediums. Continue on in this section to look at tools to get you started with presentation basics.

PRESENTATION BASICS

Get started with the basics outlined below. The following information can be useful for both teaching and for assessing presentation skills. A version of the information below is available as a free, printable poster online at www.pblconsulting.org.

I Select The Best Presentation Format

Investigate the various formats, tools and software available to you. Consider which format would be the best, given the message, the target audience, the forum and other constraints.

I Organize My Ideas

Present your message in an order that flows, with a clear beginning, middle and end. Transition with connections, segues, linking words, phrases and questions.

I Present Clearly

Present with strong voice, eye contact, body language and presence. Practice and rehearse to improve your physical presence

I Explain My Ideas

Determine your core message. Explain it succinctly, clearly and with enthusiasm. Hook the audience with an engaging introduction. End with a conclusion that leaves viewers wanting more.

I Use Media To Improve The Presentation

Use varied media - images, video, sound effects, illustrations, graphics, and more - to create interest and intrigue. Keep it simple. Incorporate text in small doses, if a viewer can't read text within 10 seconds, you've added too much.

I Answer Questions Clearly

Anticipate questions viewers might ask prior to your presentation. Develop thoughtful responses in advance. Stay flexible during Q & As.

TEACHING THE PRESENTATION BASICS

Presentation can be fun to teach and, like with the other 4 Cs, it can be dovetailed into the teaching and exploration of academic learning outcomes. Here are some fun ideas to get you started with teaching presentation.

Assess Sample Presentations

Tackling a unit on biology? Planning to share a TED talk, or something comparable, to students on the academic topics being explored? Perfect! Use that content in two ways. First, to deepen and enrich the learning experience in terms of the content, concepts and topics being addressed. Second, ask students to assess those presentations for the quality of the presentation materials and style of delivery. Try to find and use the best presentations the internet has to offer, and some less-than-stellar ones too!

Rehearse

If only words sounded as good coming out of our mouth as they sounded in our heads... I find both kids and adults are reluctant to practice a presentation out loud when rehearsing. This is necessary. And for that matter. Get out a timer and a video camera and work to refine the clarity and reduce the length of your message.

Practice What You Preach

Model, model, model. Presentation requires risk taking. If you want students to dive down the rabbit's hole, then you should take the first leap. I used to deliver a presentation during every unit or project in which student were being asked to present. I would ensure my presentation had some strengths, and some intentional flaws. Welcome to "grade the teacher" day in class. Students used our presentation rubric to grade me. As a result, we had a lively discussion about the quality of my presentation, the topics being addressed in the project or unit as well as the criteria in our rubric. I've never been able to get students more involved in analysing the details of a rubric, than when they first got to use it on their teacher.

Leverage Experts

You may not have mastered the entire scope of presentation tools and software at our fingertips. That's ok; few have! Survey students in and out of your class and leverage their varying experience and expertise with different tools and programs. Seek out real-world professionals to push into the classroom in person, or digitally, to lead workshops, offer feedback and more.

Use Clear Criteria

Adopt, adapt or co-construct clear criteria to provide clear expectations and targets for high quality presentations. Use this criteria to assess models to clarify what the criteria looks like in practice. Also, use it to facilitate formative assessments!

Scaffold a Presentation Prep Process

Consider using the presentation prep journal on the following pages that prompts students to take steps to meet each of the presentations basics. This can then be used as a formative tool by teachers to check in on students' progress. I wouldn't allow students to get onto a computer to develop their presentations until they had completed this. This led to better presentations, that were developed more quickly.

Seek Use & Use Feedback

Use protocols with students to ensure they get access to high qaulity feedback in the presentation development stage as well as in the rehearsal stage. There are dozens of feedback and "tuning" protocols that can improve the quality and quantity of feedback received. Model and teach students how to be receptive to feedback and how to use it to improve their work in progress.

Explore New Techniques & Styles

Mix it up by using a cool "model" for presentation. One is the PechaKucha (meaning chit-chat in Japanese) style of presentation. PechaKucha presentations focus on beautiful imagery to convey powerful messages. Pechakucha presentations are supposed to last strictly 6 minutes and 40 seconds with exactly twenty slides, each slide can only be projected for 20 seconds. Remember, constraints breed creativity. The other is the Ignite style of presentation. Communities host "Ignite" forums in which people can give Ignite talks. It's a bit like TED, but for the everyday person. Their slogan is: "Enlighten me, but make it quick." Their focus is on integrating storytelling, which is known to be a powerful medium to convey a message. Like PechaKucha, Ignite uses time and slide constraints - 20 slides, 5 minutes, 15 seconds per slide. The presentation slides are set to auto-advance with the time constraints. Play, try and practice with these fun approaches.

PRESENTATION PREP JOURNAL

I select the best presentation format.

I explain my ideas.

I organize my ideas.

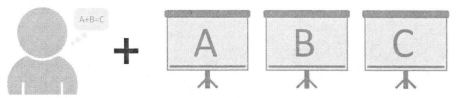

I use media to improve the presentation.

I present clearly.

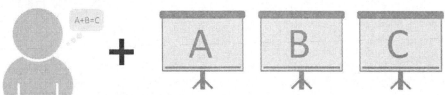

I answer questions clearly.

PRESENTATION PREP JOURNAL

I select the best presentation format: *Select the best tool(s) to create your presentation to share your message with your target audience.*

PRESENTATION SOFTWARE & TOOLS

• **Haiku Deck**
A new type of presentation software that makes telling your story "simple, beautiful and fun."
www.haikudeck.com

• **Explain Everything**
An easy to use screen-casting tool. Only available as an app.
http://www.morriscooke.com/applications-ios/explain-everything-2

• **PowerPoint**
A classic tool that helps us build presentation slides that integrates multimedia. Software available for purchase.

• **Sway**
A new tool in the Microsoft Office Suite that allows you to quickly create and share web-based presentations.

• **KeyNote**
A classic tool that helps us build presentation slides that integrate multimedia. Software available for purchase.

• **Google Presentation**
A rival to PowerPoint&KeyNote, Google Presentation lets you create slides with slightly less sophistication than PowerPoint and Keynote, but on a digital platform that allows for multi-user, real-time collaboration on a common file.

• **Prezi**
A cloud-based presentation software and storytelling tool for presenting ideas on a virtual canvas.
www.prezi.com

• **Animoto**
A tool that helps you make great videos by turning ordinary photos and video clips into stunning, HD video.www.animoto.com

• **Pictochart**
An easy, web-based infographic design application that requires very little effort to create beautiful, high quality graphics.
www.piktochart.com

I / we will use _____ and _____format for the presentation.

IGNITE	PECHAKUCHA *(chit chat in Japanese)*
Model: 5 minutes 20 slides 15 seconds per slide	**Model:** 6 minutes, forty seconds 20 slides 20 seconds per slide
Focuses on storytelling	*Focuses on captivating visual imagery*

PRESENTATION PREP JOURNAL

I explain my ideas: *Determine and elaborate on your core message.*

CORE MESSAGE	
WHY	**WHAT**
WHO	**HOW**
WHERE / WHEN	**OTHER**

PRESENTATION PREP JOURNAL

I organize my ideas: *Determine the best order to share the core message, using the storyboard below. Who will present different sections of the overall presentation.*

PRESENTATION STORYBOARD
Sketch out and organize the core message & the presenter(s) for your presentation

Presenter(s):	Presenter(s):	Presenter(s):	Presenter(s):	Presenter(s):
Presenter(s):	Presenter(s):	Presenter(s):	Presenter(s):	Presenter(s):
Presenter(s):	Presenter(s):	Presenter(s):	Presenter(s):	Presenter(s):
Presenter(s):	Presenter(s):	Presenter(s):	Presenter(s):	Presenter(s):

PRESENTATION RESOURCES

PRESENTATION PREP JOURNAL

I use media to improve my presentation: *Enhance the presentation with a variety of media.*

PRESENTATION PREP	
List any A/V aids or media you will include in your presentation	
MUSIC	AUDIO CLIPS
VIDEO	PHOTOS
DRAWINGS	OTHER

PRESENTATION PREP JOURNAL

I present clearly: *List criteria for strong presentations in the bottom box. Then, rehearse your presentation, out loud. Use the criteria to assess your delivery.*

	REHEARSAL #1	REHEARSAL #2
Strengths:		
Areas for Improvement:		

CRITERIA FOR PRESENTATION

PRESENTATION PREP JOURNAL

I answer questions clearly: *Consider questions your audience might ask. Prepare mutually agreed upon responses. Remain flexible with actual Q & As.*

ANTICIPATED QUESTIONS	POSSIBLE RESPONSES

PRESENTATION PREP JOURNAL

FEEDBACK ON PRESENTATION	**Likes**	
	Areas for Improvement	
	Other Feedback	
FEEDBACK ON MESSAGE	**Likes**	
	Areas for Improvement	
	Other Feedback	

REFLECT & CONNECT

Why bother teaching presentation skills?

What are these skills exactly?

What have you learned about how to develop presentation skills?

About assessing them?

How would you use the resources for presentation in your own practice?

Respond to this key question from your perspective as a teacher:

How can I teach and assess presentation skills?

Misconceptions About Inquiry: Often when we think of inquiry, we think of posing questions to and with students and then "letting them go." As teachers, we often feel like if we engage with students during an inquiry process, then we are "cheating on inquiry" because inquiry means that students must figure everything out on their own. To the contrary, these commonly held beliefs about inquiry are not true. They are misconceptions. Inquiry does not mean "just letting students go" or "figuring out everything on your own." That would be abandonment, not inquiry. And as we all fear, that would result in ineffective learning for most students and could also result in disorganization, even chaos, time wasted and the perpetuation of the false notion that inquiry means "hands off."

What is Inquiry? After reviewing dozens of different, and sometime overly complex or oversimplified definitions of inquiry, and after reviewing dozens of different methods of inquiry (*see seven different methods on pages 70-71*), it is clear that each method of inquiry is unique and distinct from the others. Yet, the methods also have much in common one another. In the face of these distinctions and similarities, how can we capture the essence of inquiry?

Inquiry Defined: Attempting to resolve that which is unresolved, using a process.

> ❝ Inquiry is attempting to resolve that which is unresolved, using a process. ❞

Why Inquiry? I couldn't imagine a more vital set of tools to equip any human being with than the tools of inquiry. At its core, inquiry is purposeful learning and purposeful creation, production and doing with what is learned. This is the core essence of living and doing. Life is full of novelty, ambiguity, surprises, uncertainty, and problems - everything that is "unresolved."

Inquiry as a Toolbox: Inquiry can be seen as a toolbox - a toolbox is full of tools that help us resolve that which is unresolved. Different toolboxes are useful in the face of different jobs. How would an underwater  welder be able to "resolve" his underwater welding task with, say, a carpenter's toolbox? Not well. The opposite would also be true, a carpenter would struggle to craft a table - a resolution - with the toolbox of an underwater welder. This is one of the reasons why there are so many methods of inquiry. It turns out nearly every discipline has crafted and refined its own unique method, or version, of inquiry which then becomes the process used to help individuals attempt to resolve that which is unresolved in that discipline. Different methods of inquiry are toolboxes, each is uniquely tweaked to better suit attempts at addressing the unresolved in the various disciplines, contexts and domains.

Most Disciplines Use Their Own Version of Inquiry. The method of inquiry with which we are most familiar is the Scientific Method. This would be the method, or version, of inquiry that becomes the process used by scientists to attempt to resolve that which is unresolved. What are scientists attempting to resolve? The purpose of the Scientific Method is to discover new truths about the natural world. Thus "new truths" would be the resolution of that which is unresolved for scientists. In other words, scientists make observations about our natural world and when they cannot yet explain what they observe, they inquire using the Scientific Method as a process to explain unknowns. This is just one, of many unique and distinct methods of inquiry, each suited to be useful as the key process used by practitioners in each respective discipline. There are many more methods of inquiry. Linguists have their own unique method. Anthropologists have their own unique method, and so on and so forth.

Inquiry in the Medical Field. Doctors use inquiry in their day-to-day practice. A patient arrives with an issue - something that is unresolved. The doctor attempts to resolve it using a process of inquiry. They gather information sensorily, through tests, through dialog with the patient and more. Depending on the complexity of the unresolved issue, they may be able to interpret the information in conjunction with their knowledge base in order to reach resolution easily. Resolution would include a diagnosis, a prognosis and a treatment plan for the patient. For more nuanced issues, rarer maladies or atypical presentations, a great doctor would continue gathering and interpreting information from a variety of sources. They might confer and collaborate with other doctors and specialists to discuss comparable cases and more. Doctors didn't always practice medicine in this way. There was once a time, really not so long ago, during which doctors approached the practice of medicine with a much more standardized approach. Practices around disease treatment, medication usage, child birth and more were highly standardized. Not only were these standardized practices often inhumane, but they were also often ineffective and led to many poor health outcomes for patients. Now, standardization in medicine wasn't the result of poor or malicious practitioners, rather it was the result of medicine being taught in a standardized, rote fashion, in medical schools. This realization between the link between pedagogy and style of practice led to a change in how medicine was taught to students in universities medical schools in the 60s and 70s. Two universities led the charge to start using PBL - problem-based learning, which is widely held to be an inquiry-based method - to teach medical students. Their goal was to empower students to learn how to learn, using a case study approach. Medical students were presented with a case study - a patient with an unresolved issue. Medical students then had to determine what they already knew that was relevant, what they needed to know, how they'd find out and how they'd interpret all of that information to achieve resolution - a diagnosis, a prognosis and a treatment plan. At the time, this approach was revolutionary and, as you can imagine, widely and vehemently contested.

PBL Is Now Common In Higher Education. Flash forward fifty years to today - many, if not most, university medical and dental schools have adopted this approach to teaching and doctor preparation. The practice of medicine has become increasingly adaptive and patient-centered to the extent that we are on a precipice of personalizing medicine to a degree that would have been considered science-fiction not long ago. The same shift is happening in schools and the field of education. We are moving from a standardized model to a personalized model. We are moving from standard practices, based on the "statistics" of a child - age, gender, performance data, etc. - to a flexible, learner-centric model. Importantly, we have realized that "covering content" - teaching a scope of knowledge and facts without opportunities to authentically apply, do, produce and create does not work to promote real, deep learning. Even most students who are "successful" playing this superficial game have no idea *why* they are learning what it is that they are learning. Overwhelmingly, this "coverage" approach leads to ill-prepared youngsters with a host of problems - lack of confidence, rigidness, superficial knowledge, lack of passion and more.

INQUIRY AT A GLANCE
WHY, WHAT & HOW?

Inquiry is life, life is learning and learning is inquiry. Life isn't full of neatly packaged right answers. Most of the time, there is not a clear "right answer." Even where there is a "right answer," determining how, when and to what we apply that right answer isn't clear, obvious or easy. It would be challenging to find a job where you show up, memorize information, take a test and clock-out. Either that job doesn't exist, or if it does, it's probably pretty lame and nothing I'd want my students or my own child to aspire to. Furthermore, that job will likely become automated in the near future. As a teacher and as a parent, I'd rather focus my efforts on teaching youngsters *how to think*, in lieu of *what to think*. Inquiry is a structure for thinking, learning and dealing with life's inherent open-endedness. While I don't know what students will *specifically* face in their post-secondary lives and in their futures, I am *absolutely certain* that they will face novelty. They will face ambiguity. They will face unpredictable and complex problems. Having a set of facts and right answers alone will not serve them. What will serve them is extensive practice learning through a variety of methods of inquiry, in the face of ill-structured problems and open-ended questions. What will serve them is the mindset of a curious learner, equipped with the toolboxes of inquiry, who possesses practice using the tools in each toolbox.

Think back to the toolbox metaphor. While carpenters each use a carpenter's toolbox, each individual carpenter's toolbox is unique and distinct. Over time, a carpenter adds new tools, learns to use tools better and even fails, at times, to achieve resolution on a project with an existing set of tools. The same is true of inquiry. Those new to the Scientific Method, or any other method of inquiry, will need practice with that toolbox to become increasingly adept at using it to achieve resolutions in the face of that which is unresolved. This is why university medical schools shifted their approach to teaching medicine. They recognized that pre-med students needed this authentic practice, before they launched into the profession. Why prepare students for life and careers in a way that is different than the way they would actually need to be, do, act and think well in life? Why prepare students for life, by learning to memorize and regurgitate facts? That is not what they will do in their lives. So, let's do real work now.

Inquiry must be practiced. Though different methods can be learned and practiced, even they unravel differently in the face of different unresolved issues, problems, questions and unknowns. My good friend and colleague once told me that, "every process eventually breaks down once you're deep enough into the work." She's a high school science teacher at an internationally-renowned school that practices PBL. And she's absolutely right.

72

Getting Started. First, a few words of encouragement. Perhaps you are concerned that you, yourself, lack experience with the toolboxes of inquiry. That's ok, start by starting. You can learn and practice alongside students. If we want students to embrace learning and become lifelong-learners, then we must model that spirit ourselves. How could we ask them to do something that is new and possibly uncomfortable, if we are unwilling to do it ourselves?

Start by starting.

Inquiry Basics. Even though there are a variety of different inquiry methods, each method shares the same fundamental components - attempting to resolve that which is unresolved by using what you know, determining what you need to know, learning new information and interpreting everything in an effort to resolve. Typically, you bounce around the various phases, as much as needed, until resolution is achieved. Sometimes resolving one thing, leads to the realization that you now recognize a dozen new (new-to-you, at least) unresolved things.

That which is unresolved could be any of the following: a design challenge, an engineering design challenge, a threat, a problem (no not a simple math problem, an ill-structured and ideally authentic problem to which there is not a clear right answer), a decision to-be-made, a request for services, a need, a controversial issue, unexplained observations about the natural world, a dilemma, and more. As you may have already considered, there is a powerful opportunity to inspire the "unresolved" starting point from our students themselves! We can co-construct open-ended questions, relevant problems and other "unresolved" springboards with our students. Certainly there is plenty of known information and there is indeed value in learning existing knowledge. Inquiry does not exclude the act of learning existing knowledge. In fact, that's the second phase - use what you already know, determine what you need to know and learn that. So, learning existing knowledge is important, is allowed and is fundamentally a part of inquiry. However, in inquiry, learning existing knowledge is not an end in itself but rather a means to a new end - a resolution of that which was unresolved. An inquiry process may lead to student-created resolutions that could be any of the following: new scientific findings, new conclusions, new accounts of the past, original theories, proofs, solutions, designs, engineered devices, decisions, plans of action, campaigns, positions and more. The key with resolutions is that they are NEW. They didn't exist before. So, if the end result of "inquiry" is that a student learns a set of facts or existing knowledge, then it's actually not inquiry. That's actually just rote learning masquerading as inquiry. Inquiry must result in attempts at NEW, original resolutions.

You Can Help Students Where They'll Struggle. Because students are often so used to learning and repeating what they learned, they may struggle with moving from the second phase of inquiry that focuses on learning, to the third phase of interpreting what has been learned in order to resolve. This is where they'll likely need the most support from the teacher.

METHODS OF FOCUSED INQUIRY

QUESTION: How are these methods the same and different?

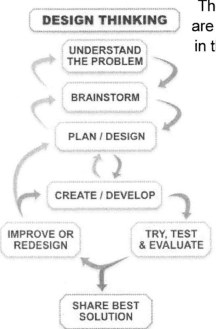

These two methods of inquiry are fairly similar. They are used in the adult world by designers and by engineers to conceptualize, plan, create and improve new "things" that have value.

Increasingly, teachers, students and schools at all levels are using these methods, which are already common in industry, to frame a process for making and creating.

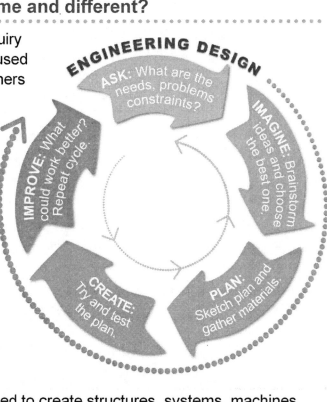

Generally speaking, the Engineering Design Cycle is used to create structures, systems, machines, engines & code. Design Thinking handles everything else.

The Historical Method is used by historians to write new accurate accounts of the past.

The purpose of the Scientific Method is to discover "new truths" about the natural world.

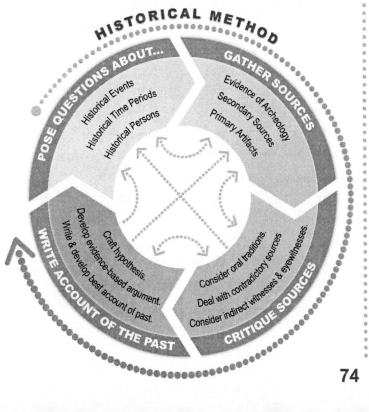

THE SCIENTIFIC METHOD

OBSERVE, QUESTION, WONDER
Look at the world around you. Why are things the way they are?

TRY TO EXPLAIN
Interpret your observations and conduct preliminary research.

CRAFT HYPOTHESIS
If you can't explain your observations, develop a possible explanation.

TEST HYPOTHESIS
Design and carry out an experiment.

INTERPRET RESULTS
Make sense of observations and collected data from experiment.

REPORT FINDINGS
Draw and share conclusions in the best way to whom they matter.

METHODS OF FOCUSED INQUIRY

INQUIRY DEFINED: Attempting to resolve that which is unresolved, using a process.

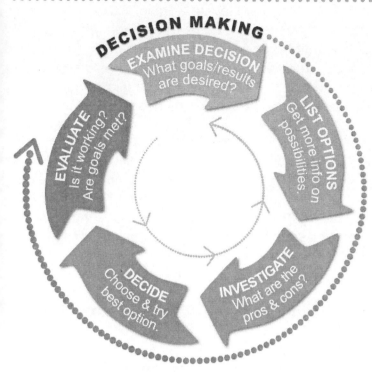

DECISION MAKING

- **EXAMINE DECISION** What goals/results are desired?
- **LIST OPTIONS** Get more info on possibilities.
- **INVESTIGATE** What are the pros & cons?
- **DECIDE** Choose & try best option.
- **EVALUATE** Is it working? Are goals met?

As the pattern reveals, many of these methods are used within specific disciplinary domains. Open-ended inquiry is "non-discipline specific" method. It could also be called "Generic Inquiry." Using this method is a great option if your project doesn't ask learners to take on an "adult-world professional role." E.g. Acting like a historian, scientist or engineer.

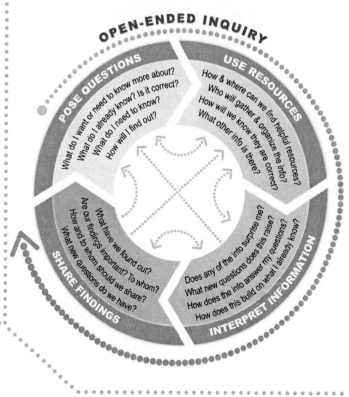

OPEN-ENDED INQUIRY

- **POSE QUESTIONS** What do I want or need to know more about? What do I already know? Is it correct? What do I need to know? How will I find out?
- **USE RESOURCES** How & where can we find helpful resources? Who will gather & organize the info? How will we know they are correct? What other info is there?
- **INTERPRET INFORMATION** Does any of the info surprise me? What new questions does this raise? How does the info answer my questions? How does this build on what I already know?
- **SHARE FINDINGS** What have we found out? Are our findings important? To whom? How and to whom should we share? What new questions do we have?

We all make decisions on a daily basis, but rarely do we carefully use a decision making process, like this one. Imagine the world we'd live in if we all did!

This process is most often used in the fields of politics, business, marketing and military strategy.

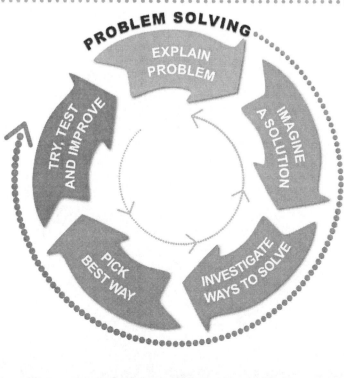

PROBLEM SOLVING

- **EXPLAIN PROBLEM**
- **IMAGINE A SOLUTION**
- **INVESTIGATE WAYS TO SOLVE**
- **PICK BEST WAY**
- **TRY, TEST AND IMPROVE**

Other than "open-ended inquiry," this problem solving process may be the most "disciplinarily-neutral" method available. Just think, there is no and seemingly never will be a shortage of real-world problems. This is true in every thinkable discipline and domain.

John Dewey even posited that, "we only think when we are confronted with problems." As a pragmatist, he believed the goal of thinking was to guide how to act well within our world and lives.

Find these free graphics & journals at www.pblconsulting.org

DESIGN THINKING AT A GLANCE

Design Thinking Is the Go-To Method of Inquiry for Designers. Additionally, it can and is used in other contexts, fields and disciplines. It is a process to prototype, create and innovate. Typically, designers would use this method when presented with open-ended design challenges. It helps designers conceptualize, plan, create and improve new things that have value - consumer goods, inventions, art, design esthetics, concept designs, etc. - for a target audience. It is intended to be rapid. Sometimes it acts as the structure for a start-to-finish design process that might last only a day, a few hours, or less. In design, time is often considered a more valuable resource than money. So, starting and failing fast is the name of the game.

Everyone Should Learn Design Thinking. Design Thinking helps shift mindsets. From consumer mindsets, to producer mindsets. From accepting mindsets, to questioning mindsets. From passive mindsets, to active and empowered mindsets. I recently heard a colleague say that everyone, no matter their field or discipline, should learn to think like a Designer. Design Thinking is being used in the lower elementary grades, in middle school, in high school, in higher education and certainly in industry. Increasingly, teachers, students and schools at all levels are using Design Thinking to tackle challenges linked to various disciplines. In order words, students could learn about biology - for example, plant and animal adaptations and more - as they respond to a biomimicry design challenge using Design Thinking.

Phases of Design Thinking - There are five key phases, outlined in this Design Thinking Poster. The structure is designed to be iterative, meaning repetitive and non-linear within the phases. Backtracking is encouraged!

Phase 1 - Understand the parameters of the design challenge itself. Should involve empathizing with the end user experience.

Phase 2 - Brainstorm possibilities using actual brainstorming methods and techniques. (*See pages 28-30.*)

Phase 3 - Plan, design and/or sketch ideas and possibilities. Use them to uncover problems and/or seek feedback.

Phase 4 - Prototype. Cycle through the three components of this phase as needed until you've arrived at a viable solution. Toss out ideas freely. Celebrate going backward to fetch earlier ideas as well as simply starting from scratch.

Phase 5 - Share best solutions in the best ways when and to whom they matter.

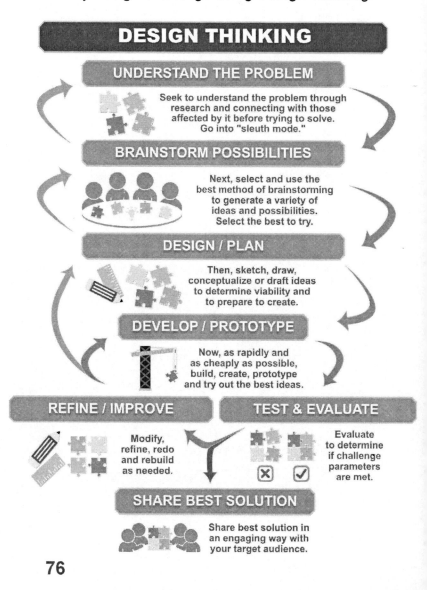

DESIGN THINKING

UNDERSTAND THE PROBLEM
Seek to understand the problem through research and connecting with those affected by it before trying to solve. Go into "sleuth mode."

BRAINSTORM POSSIBILITIES
Next, select and use the best method of brainstorming to generate a variety of ideas and possibilities. Select the best to try.

DESIGN / PLAN
Then, sketch, draw, conceptualize or draft ideas to determine viability and to prepare to create.

DEVELOP / PROTOTYPE
Now, as rapidly and as cheaply as possible, build, create, prototype and try out the best ideas.

REFINE / IMPROVE
Modify, refine, redo and rebuild as needed.

TEST & EVALUATE
Evaluate to determine if challenge parameters are met.

SHARE BEST SOLUTION
Share best solution in an engaging way with your target audience.

DESIGN THINKING JOURNAL

PHASE 1 - UNDERSTAND THE PROBLEM: In this phase, we seek to better understand the problem itself. Consider the following questions to better understand the parameters of the design challenge.

WHAT?	WHY?

WHEN? FOR HOW LONG?	WHERE?

WITH WHOM?	FOR WHOM?

STRENGTHS / CHALLENGES?	ADDITIONAL THINGS TO CONSIDER?

Find these free resources at www.pblconsulting.org

DESIGN THINKING JOURNAL

PHASE 2 - BRAINSTORM: Select the best method of brainstorming for your challenge, task or problem. Select a facilitator, as needed, and get started!

Brainstorming Rules of Engagement:
1. Generate As Many Ideas As Possible, As Quickly As Possible
2. Piggyback on Shared Ideas
3. Suspend Judgement, of Yourself and of Others
4. Be Fearless - Wild, Wacky and Zany Ideas Are Encouraged
5. Get Comfortable With Silence - Ideas Can Come In Waves, Do At Least Three Waves

 Designate a team member to keep track of the number of unique ideas!

DESIGN THINKING JOURNAL

PHASE 3 - PLAN / DESIGN: Review your ideas from the brainstorm session. Pick the best ones and sketch out some preliminary designs.

 Now, based on the sketches and concepts, select the most promising idea(s) to develop, produce and prototype. Do others agree with which design ideas should be pursued?

DESIGN THINKING JOURNAL

PHASE 4: PROTOTYPE - In this phase, cycle actively through the following components: (1) Create / Develop, (2) Try, Test, Evaluate and (3) Improve and/or Redesign. Remember to celebrate failures by learning from them, and return to earlier phases liberally, without judgement.

	DESCRIBE IT	TEST IT - LOG RESULTS	FIX IT OR DITCH IT? DESCRIBE NEXT STEP
FIRST DESIGN/ DRAFT			
SECOND DESIGN/ DRAFT			
THIRD DESIGN/ DRAFT			
FOURTH DESIGN/ DRAFT			

DESIGN THINKING JOURNAL

PHASE 5: SHARE BEST SOLUTION - In this phase, determine the best way to share your best solution(s) to whom they matter. Consider the following questions to determine the best ways to share.

Target audience: To whom is your solution relevant?	
What is the best medium and media for sharing your solution with your target audience? **Why is this the best?**	
When would be the best time frame to share? **Why is this the best?**	
How could you best share "the why" behind your solution? **How could you best share "the what" behind your solution?**	
Given additional time, resources and materials, how could you improve your solution?	
Reflect on your process. Would you change your process in future design challenges?	

PROBLEM SOLVING AT A GLANCE

Problem Solving is Not Linked to a Specific Discipline. Other than "open-ended inquiry," this problem solving process may be the most "discipline-neutral" method available. Just think, there is no and seemingly never will be a shortage of real-world problems. This is true in every thinkable discipline and domain. John Dewey even posited that, "we only think when we are confronted with problems." As a pragmatist, he believed the goal of thinking was to guide how to act well within our world and lives.

You can find multiple problem solving processes, some with five key phases, some with additional steps. As you may remember, this is linked to critical thinking because it can be considered a thinking strategy - a process one can learn, practice and systematize as approach to addressing ambiguous situations and ill-structured problems. Thinking strategies are one of the important domains of capacity that can be developed to build critical thinkers.

Steps in Problem Solving - There are five key steps, outlined in this Problem Solving infographic. However, you can find multiple problem solving processes, some with five key steps, and others with additional steps.

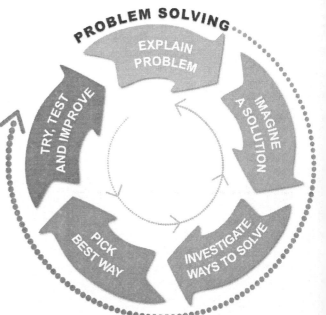

Step 1 - In the first phase, we critically analyze or "unpack" the problem itself. This may start from a problem statement that we unpack into its component parts. Or, in the absence of a clear problem statement, we start by analyzing all of the components of the problem. This can result in problem statement. Let's take the problem of recurring headaches, for example. I would need to name the problem and the following components: intensity, frequency, duration, known triggers, causes, or antecedents, etc. I'd need to think about how long ago they started and what else what happening around that time. LOTS to consider, and this can be outlined into a problem statement.

Step 2 - I love this phase in problem solving - before trying or starting to solve, we must first imagine a solution. All of the elements of the problem that we just named and quantified, we can now imagine what they'd look like in a solution. This creates a set of criteria that we can later use to evaluate our attempts at solving the problem. Back to the headache example, does "solving" look like eliminating all headaches, forever in my future. Probably not. Rather, I'd go component by component and quantify a "solution" level.

Step 3 - In this phase, we investigate possible ways to solve. This typically involves research and learning about best practices. It's very unlikely that we are the first to attempt to solve any problem. So, what has been tried before us? What worked? How do we know? This can be trickier than it sounds because problems can be nuanced. Take the headaches example. There are different types, causes and parameters around treatment. Often we have to go back to unpack the problem even more in this stage.

Step 4 - Of all of the possible solution pathways, which one fits the best with the nuances of the problem? This phase is a bit of a matching game.

Step 5 - Now we try out our proposed solution and assess the results. We can use the criteria from phase 2. We can seek to learn from both successes and failures in order to improve.

PROBLEM SOLVING JOURNAL

Step 1 - Explain the Problem: Use the following prompts to help you write and elaborate on a problem statement.

What is the problem?	
What are some of the possible causes?	
What is the frequency of the problem? **Intensity?**	
When did it start? What else happened around the time that it started?	
How long has the problem been occurring?	
Now put all the information from the above boxes together in order to write a succinct problem statement.	

PROBLEM SOLVING JOURNAL

Step 2 - Imagine a Solution: Use the following prompts to help you write a solutions statement.

Frequency	
Duration	
Intensity	
Amount	
Treatability	
Other metric:	
Other metric:	
Other metric:	
What would it look like if the problem were solved?	

 Metric: Any type of measurement used to gauge some quantifiable component

PROBLEM SOLVING JOURNAL

Step 3 - Investigate Ways To Solve: Conduct research to learn about best practices in solving the problem to the level defined in your solution statement.

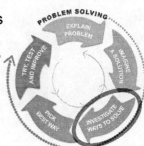

> **Conduct research to determine what are the best practices in solving this type of problem.**

Brainstorm possible solutions based on the information found, reviewed and learned.

PROBLEM SOLVING JOURNAL

Step 4 - Pick the Best Way: Consider all of your research and all of your ideas so far to select the best possible solutions. Consider the questions below as you justify why a possible solution is the best one.

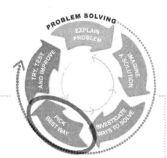

Based on your analysis thus far, what is the most promising idea?	
Why do you believe it will help you achieve your solutions criteria?	
What do you need to be able to implement your idea?	
Other things to consider?	

PROBLEM SOLVING JOURNAL

Step 5 - Try, Test & Evaluate: What is your plan to implement and evaluate your idea to solve your problem?

When, frequency, duration?	
Who is involved?	
How will you evaluate? **When, how often, etc.**	
What materials do you need?	
Other implementation considerations	

ENGINEERING DESIGN AT A GLANCE

The Engineering Design Cycle is the Method of Inquiry Used By Engineers. This method of inquiry is specific to the domain of engineering and is used by engineers to create systems, engines, motors, machines, materials, structures, code and more. It's also used in aviation. If you are creating something else, and that thing doesn't require mathematical calculations to ensure integrity and safety, then it's possible that Design Thinking is a better fit.

Phases in the Engineering Design Cycle - There are five key phases to the engineering design cycle. They are outlined in the Engineering Design infographic. As one of my friends, who is an engineer, said, "this [the Engineering Design Cycle] can be used to engineer anything - from a nut, or a bolt, to a semi-truck."

Phase 1 - ASK. In the first phase, engineers begin by outlining that which is unresolved. In the case of engineers, this would typically be a need for something. They determine what problems occurring around this need and what constraints are they working under. Constraints could include time, materials, budget, existing technology, size, code and more. Remember, constraints aren't necessarily seen as bad, or negative in the realm of engineering, art, design, etc. Rather, constraints just exist, and clarifying them, helps us produce a framework in which to achieve any given resolution.

Phase 2 - IMAGINE. Now that we have a framework, we can imagine a wide variety of possible ideas to pursue.

Phase 3 - PLAN. Get started with the best ideas by developing a clear plan. This could include creating sketches, blueprints and possibly procedures. It also includes determining the necessary materials, tools, machines, people and space to engineer a prototype and then a first article.

ENGINEERING DESIGN

ASK: What are the needs, problems constraints?

IMAGINE: Brainstorm ideas and choose the best one.

PLAN: Sketch plan and gather materials.

CREATE: Try and test the plan.

IMPROVE: What could work better? Repeat cycle.

Phase 4 - CREATE. The emphasis in engineering is to fail fast and fail early. This means, the faster they can get a prototype the better. This is because a prototype can provide better insight into what works, and what doesn't work, so that it can be fixed, faster. Often there are multiple prototypes, each requiring engineers to step into the fifth phase to determine how to improve and then possibly into to the earlier phases to ask, imagine and plan accordingly. When they arrive at their first working prototype - that's a first article. And that too can be improved.

Phase 5 - IMPROVE. The emphasis in this phase is to analyze both successes and failures to determine how to improve that which is being engineered.

Phase 1 - ASK: What are the needs, problems and constraints?

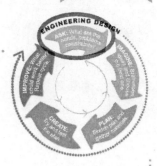

Phase 2 - IMAGINE: Brainstorm ideas and choose the best one.

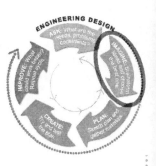

Phase 3 - PLAN: Sketch plan and gather materials.

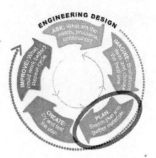

ENGINEER'S NOTEBOOK

Phase 4 - CREATE: Try and test the plan.

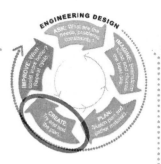

Phase 5 - IMPROVE: What could work better? Repeat cycle.

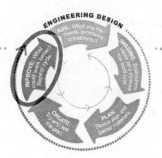

Decision Making is Useful Both for Individuals Personally and in Some Professions. We all make decisions on a daily basis, but rarely do we carefully use a decision making process, like this one. Imagine the world we would live in if we all did use a careful decision making process like this!

This process is most often used in the fields of politics, business, marketing and military strategy. Like problem solving, the decision making process could also be linked to critical thinking because it can be considered a thinking strategy - a process one can learn, practice and systematize as approach to addressing ambiguous situations and ill-structured problems. Thinking strategies are one of the five domains of capacity that can be developed to build critical thinkers.

Steps in Decision Making - There are five key steps, outlined in this Decision Making infographic. However, you can find multiple decision making processes, some with five key steps, and others with additional steps.

Step 1 - Examine The Decision To Be Made. We begin the process of making a decision by thinking of the end in mind. What are we hoping to achieve? What goals are we hoping to meet? What results or outcomes are desired?

Step 2 - List Options. Now we can first list all the options before us, which may require some, or even extensive, research.

Step 3 - Investigate. - Once we have the gamut of possible decisions, we can actively consider each of them. We can weigh the pros and cons. We can pro-actively think of likely consequences and of possible "unintended consequences" This is a bit like chess, where the board is dynamic, there are multiple variables in play and usually no decision has clear-cut results.

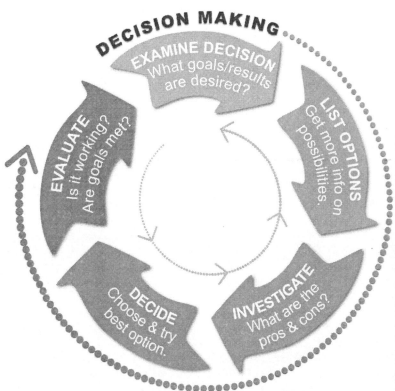

Step 4 - Decide. - Given the options, and our careful consideration of the merits of the options, step four is when we make a decision and put it into action.

Step 5 - Evaluate. - Finally, we can ask ourselves how the decision is working. How do we measure if it's working? Well, we have to return to the desired goals, results and outcomes identified in Step 1. Are those being attained? How do we know? Did unintended consequences occur that need to be addressed? This evaluation process may lead to adjustments to the action that had been decided upon and even to new decisions that may need to be made.

The journal on the subsequent pages can be used to guide students through each step of the process. The journal is available Online, in an editable format at - www.pblconsulting.org - in the Free Resources section, in the Inquiry Resources sub-page.

DECISION MAKING JOURNAL

Step 1 - Examine the Decision: What goals/results are desired?

Step 2 - List Options: Get more info on the possibilities.

DECISION MAKING JOURNAL

Step 3 - Investigate: What are the pros and cons?

DECISION MAKING JOURNAL

Step 4 - Decide: Choose and try best option.

Step 5 - Evaluate: Is it working? Are goals met? Repeat cycle, as needed.

Open-Ended Inquiry Is Not Specific to a Discipline. Open-ended inquiry could also be called "generic inquiry" or even "non-discipline-specific" inquiry. It is "discipline-neutral." Now the word "generic" could be seen as having a bit of a negative connotation. The term "generic" is certainly lackluster. However, there is nothing negative about Open Ended Inquiry. Sometimes great inquiry starts with questions and curiosities that can be explored in an open-ended manner. That is quite lovely actually.

With many of the other methods, a person using that method either actually is a professional working in the disciplinary domain in which that method was developed, or are "acting like" a practitioner in that disciplinary domain. In other words, if I'm using the Engineering Design Cycle, I'm either actually an engineer, or I'm acting like an engineer. So, a history teacher might use Open Ended Inquiry with students, in a history project. Why not use the Historical Method? Well, perhaps you're not framing a unit or a project in a way that asks students to "act like a historian." There's nothing wrong with that. Perhaps you're a science teacher launching a unit or a project, that is not framed in a way that asks students to "act like a scientist." That might be entirely appropriate. So, if you're not asking your students to "act like" an engineer, a scientist, a historian, etc. then you might look to structure an inquiry process using this model of "Open-Ended Inquiry."

Again, this method is also linked to critical thinking because it can be considered a thinking strategy - a process that one can learn, practice and systematize as approach to addressing ambiguous situations and ill-structured problems. Thinking strategies are one of the important domains of capacity that can be developed to build critical thinkers.

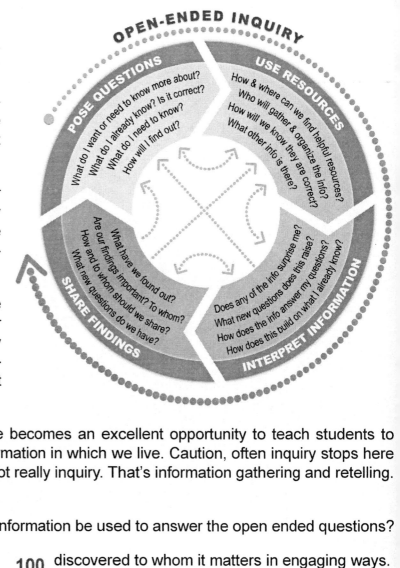

Phases in Open Ended Inquiry - There are four phases outlined in the Open Ended Inquiry infographic shown here. However, there are variations of this model that are also "non-discipline-specific" that can be found and used.

Phase 1 - Pose Questions. This is where we explore our curiosities. What do we want or need to learn more about? What do we already know and is it correct? Be sure to ask open-ended level two and three questions that require more than just knowledge to answer.

Phase 2 - Find and Use Resources. This phase becomes an excellent opportunity to teach students to become better navigators of the ocean of information in which we live. Caution, often inquiry stops here and students retell what they've found. That' not really inquiry. That's information gathering and retelling. Help them move into the next step.

Phase 3 - Interpret Information. How can the information be used to answer the open ended questions?

Phase 4 - Share Findings. Share what you've discovered to whom it matters in engaging ways.

OPEN ENDED JOURNAL

Phase 1 - Pose Questions

What do I want or need to know more about?

What do I already know? Is it correct?

What do I need to know?

How will I find out?

OPEN ENDED JOURNAL

Phase 2 - Use Information & Resources

How & where can we find helpful resources?

Who will gather & organize the info.

How will we know they are correct?

What other info is there?

Phase 3 - Interpret Information

How does this build on what I already know?	
How does the info answer my questions?	
What new questions does this raise?	
Does any of the info surprise me?	

Phase 4 - Share Findings

What new questions do
we have?

How and to whom should
we share?

Are our findings important?
To whom?

What have we found out?

HISTORICAL METHOD AT A GLANCE

The Historical Method is the Method of Inquiry Used By Historians. This method of inquiry is specific to historians and the resolution that comes at the end is an "accurate" written account of the past. I put accurate in quotations because history is not so cut and dry. I can barely give you an accurate account of my entire day yesterday. Couples fail to give accurate accounts when recalling the details of an argument. So, where does written history come from? Historians learn, practice and use a method of inquiry that helps them interpret the past as fairly and accurately as possible. The method prompts them to use a variety of sources, to critically analyze those sources, to weigh and rank source credibility and more. Ultimately, their written account of the past begins with a hypothesis - yes, a hypothesis - that they support with evidence. History is qualitative and interpretive. Just like with the scientific method, our shift needs to be from teaching the "facts" of history, to learning the tools to interpret history for ourselves. The "facts" outlined in a given book, textbook or other written account are actually not facts. They are one or more historians' interpretations of the past. There may be other interpretations that vary slightly, or substantially.

To illustrate the idea that history is subject to interpretation, I did a quick search on Amazon for "JFK biography, in books" and I quickly counted over a dozen different biographies for JFK. I'm sure many of them rest in strong agreement on a lot of matters. Perhaps they sometimes convey a nearly identical slice

of the past. I'd also wager to say that they sometimes vary to large degrees on their interpretation of JFK's life, time as president and more. So is one right, and another wrong? Not at all, history is qualitative and interpretive. Interestingly, each biography had a slightly different lens focusing on a unique aspect of JFK's bio. One was entitled, "JFK's Last Hundred Days" and was zooming in just on that short period of time. Another was entitled, "JFK and the Masculine Mystique." The point is that in the first phase of the Historical Method, we are asked to pose questions about historical events, time periods and persons. The quality of our questions matter. If we pose, "who was the 35th president.?" Then, inquiry has never begun. If we pose genuine curiosities and unknowns about the past, then we can start digging. I bet we'd learn a lot of those "facts," and much, more. Importantly, we'd also learn about how to learn and interpret the past for ourselves.

Phase 1 - Pose Questions. Start with curiosities and questions about past people, events and time periods.

Phase 2 - Gather Sources. This is where the real work begins gathering any of the following sources that are available - primary artifacts, evidence of archeology, a variety of secondary sources, oral tradition, indirect witnesses, eyewitnesses and more.

Phase 3 - Critique Sources. Not all sources are created equal. In a trial for example, a judge may counsel the jury to rank the weight of testimony based on the credibility of a given witness. Sources can be interpreted in different ways and can even contradict one another. There are procedures to deal with this.

Phase 4 - Write Account of the Past. Based on all of the information, historians begin to craft a hypothesis. This is essentially a preliminary synthesis of their interpretation of the evidence. They build evidence to support it and proceed to craft a written   account of the past.

HISTORICAL METHOD JOURNAL

Phase 1 - Pose Questions

Historical Events

Historical Time Periods

Historical Persons

HISTORICAL METHOD JOURNAL

Phase 2 - Gather Sources

Evidence of Archeology

Secondary Sources

Primary Artifacts

HISTORICAL METHOD JOURNAL

Phase 3 - Critique Sources

Consider indirect witnesses & eyewitnesses.

Deal with contradictory sources.

Consider oral traditions.

HISTORICAL METHOD JOURNAL

Phase 4 - Write Account of the Past

Craft hypothesis.

Develop evidence-based argument.

Write & develop best account of past.

SCIENTIFIC METHOD AT A GLANCE

Why use the Scientific Method? The purpose of the Scientific Method is to discover "new truths" about the world around us. I use the word "truths" lightly because science is more in the business of asking questions than providing answers. Scientists learn to become keen and curious observers of the natural world. They embrace the habits of mind of "responding to the world with wonderment and awe" as well as "questioning." They use the Scientific Method as a process to attempt to explain that which they observe and otherwise can't explain.

> Science is more in the business of asking questions than providing answers.

A Metaphor for the Scientific Method: Think of the scientific method as brink laying and each new scientific finding as an individual brink. Now think of the work of science as building a brink "house of truth." It's a slow process and will never really be complete - perhaps a bit like the genius and famous basilica in Barcelona, Spain by Gaudi that is still under construction after over 100 years. New bricks are laid on the foundations of bricks - discoveries - laid before them by other brick layers. Sometimes new revelations about how to create stronger bricks are made, or new techniques for how to improve the strength of a wall are discovered, and the builders and brick layers tear down entire sections of the house and rebuild them in a way that is consistent with their newfound knowledge, skills, understandings and techniques. That is what science is - a slow process of building understandings about the world around us. Importantly, science is also about questioning the understandings laid before us.

Generally speaking, the Scientific Method is not practiced or taught in this way in schools. Rather, science courses have been framed around the learning of scientific facts, or should we say previous discoveries. But only some of them. Why those? Why not others? Well kids shouldn't worry about that - just learn about these bricks over here.

Now let's switch out of this metaphor for a moment and consider real brick laying. I'm no expert in brick laying, and frankly if I were buying brinks to construct, say, a brick wall, I would have really no idea, no sense, no intuition about the variations in quality of different types of bricks. Furthermore, if I hired a brick layer to build a brick wall, I would have very little sense for whether or not it was well-built, whether or not it was solid, whether or not I should trust its integrity. To develop a better sense and ability to evaluate the quality of a brick structure, I would actually have to learn and practice brick laying myself.

Canned Science Activities Aren't Real Science - Think for a moment about the Food Network Show "Chopped." Three chefs each get a mystery box. Each box contains the same three ingredients that must be featured in dish they imagine and create, with very limited time. What is amazing about this show is that each time the chefs generate wildly **112** different dishes. This element of variety and

SCIENTIFIC METHOD AT A GLANCE

unpredictability is what creates intrigue. Imagine if instead of a mystery box, the chefs were all asked to make scalloped potatoes, with the same ingredients, in the same way, using the same process developed by a chef before them. If the competing chefs' renditions of this recipe don't come out as anticipated, they are wrong. The chefs can't vary, twist or tweak the recipe. In essence, we all know what we are going to end up with before we even begin. The result? Well, it would be a remarkably boring show.

Overwhelmingly, that is how the Scientific Method is taught in schools today. Kids do labs, with an expected outcome and a fixed set of procedures that is guided by a pre-determined question. Students derive the same findings that were already known and derived before them. Other than building fluency with procedures and acting as a model for framing experiments, these types of activities have nothing to do with the spirit of the Scientific Method. They don't give students an opportunity to observe, notice, wonder or question in an authentic way. They don't result in the production of "new knowledge."

A Note on Replication - Now, there is great importance in the replication of existing scientific studies. After all, a key premise in science, with some notable exceptions, is that one should be able to replicate the findings of any given study. Indeed, replication isn't always bad and there are some really cool projects anchored in replication. Though in these projects, students are actually selecting a study that genuinely interests them and that might not replicate the original findings. If it replicates, that's useful information. If it doesn't, we can ask why and dig deeper around the nuances between the two sets of findings. Even in this case, the process is very different than the labs mentioned above, in which everyone derives the same findings, predictably, through a formulaic process with predetermined outcomes. Again, science is more in the business of asking questions than providing answers.

The Shift Ahead of Us - What do we know? And how do we know what we know? We need to move from consuming limited and controlled amounts of scientific facts and move toward using the scientific method to produce scientific findings ourselves. Science is about our ability to intake input, using nothing more than our seven primary senses - sight, sound, taste, touch, smell, movement and body awareness - as well as other input receiving tools and devices, that we create. Then we make sense of our senses and other received input using our innate faculties of reasoning and logic, as well as tools and computational devices, that we create, in an effort to generate new knowledge and understandings. All of this is based on our curiosities, wonders, questions and observations about the world around us. That is truly amazing. We need to embrace this spirit of science - that means being curious and wondrous with kids in every single science course we offer because we need to move from being consumers of knowledge to becoming producers of knowledge.

> " We need to move from being consumers of knowledge to becoming producers of knowledge. "

THE SCIENTIFIC METHOD

OBSERVE, QUESTION, WONDER
Look at the world around you. Why are things the way they are?

TRY TO EXPLAIN
Interpret your observations and conduct preliminary research.

CRAFT HYPOTHESIS
If you can't explain your observations, develop a possible explanation.

TEST HYPOTHESIS
Design and carry out an experiment.

INTERPRET RESULTS
Make sense of observations and collected data from experiment.

REPORT FINDINGS
Draw and share conclusions in the best way to whom they matter.

SCIENTIFIC METHOD JOURNAL

Phase 1 - Observe, Question, Wonder:

Look at the world around you. Why are things the way they are?

THE SCIENTIFIC METHOD

OBSERVE, QUESTION, WONDER
Look at the world around you.
Why are things the way they are?

TRY TO EXPLAIN
Interpret your observations and
conduct preliminary research.

CRAFT HYPOTHESIS
If you can't explain your observations,
develop a possible explanation.

TEST HYPOTHESIS
Design and carry out
an experiment.

INTERPRET RESULTS
Make sense of observations and
collected data from experiment.

REPORT FINDINGS
Draw and share conclusions in
the best way to whom they matter.

SCIENTIFIC METHOD JOURNAL

Phase 2 - Try to Explain:
Interpret your observations and conduct preliminary research.

Phase 3 - Craft Hypothesis:

If you can't explain your observations, develop a possible explanation.

THE SCIENTIFIC METHOD

OBSERVE, QUESTION, WONDER
Look at the world around you.
Why are things the way they are?

TRY TO EXPLAIN
Interpret your observations and
conduct preliminary research.

CRAFT HYPOTHESIS
If you can't explain your observations,
develop a possible explanation.

TEST HYPOTHESIS
Design and carry out
an experiment.

INTERPRET RESULTS
Make sense of observations and
collected data from experiment.

REPORT FINDINGS
Draw and share conclusions in
the best way to whom they matter.

Phase 4 - Test Hypothesis:

Design and carry out an experiment.

Phase 5 - Interpret Results:

Make sense of observations and collected data from experiment.

Phase 6 - Report Findings:
Draw and share conclusions to whom they matter.

INQUIRY - WHY, WHAT & HOW?

REFLECT & CONNECT	
What is inquiry exactly? **Why bother teaching and using inquiry?**	
What have you learned about how to develop capacity with inquiry? **About assessing the inquiry process?**	
How would you use the resources for inquiry in your own practice?	
What new questions do you have about inquiry?	

Case, Roland (2005, Spring). Moving Critical Thinking to the Main Stage. Education Canada, 45(2), 45-49.

Cheng, Karen X (2013, November 26). Girl Learns to Dance in a Year - Interview [Video file]. Retrieved November 5, 2016, from YouTube: https://www.youtube.com/watch?v=IPZjhUmDSTE.

Doorley, Scott & Wittholf, Scott (2011). Make Space: How to Set the Stage for Creative Collaboration . : John Wiley & Sons, 2011.

Hill, Linda (2014, September 1). How to Manage for Collective Creativity [Video file]. Retrieved October 14, 2016, from TED Talks : www.ted.com.

Kroski, Ellyssa (2013, March 12). A Librarian's Guide to Makerspaces: 16 Resources. Open Education Database, p. 1-2. Retrieved from http://oedb.org/ilibrarian/a-librarians-guide-to-makerspaces/.

Maker Faire. (2004-2016). Retrieved October 15, 2016, from http://makerfaire.com/makerfairehistory/.

Paul, R. & Elder, L. (2006). Critical Thinking: Concepts and Tools. : The Foundation for Critical Thinking.

Robinson, Sir Ken (2010, October 1). Changing Education Paradigms [Video file]. Retrieved October 14, 2016, from TED Talks: www.ted.com.

Sherwin, David (2010). Creative Workshop: 80 Challenges to Sharpen Your Design Skills. : HOW Books, 2010.

Yang, Yu-Hsiu (2013, September 30). Maker trailer - A documentary on the Maker Movement [Video file]. Retrieved October 17, 2016, from MakerTheMovie: http://makerthemovie.com/.